Reclaimi

Dedicated to
Dr. Taeko (Hoshi) Summerville and Jeanine McMurtrie

Reclaiming Populism

How Economic Fairness Can Win Back Disenchanted Voters

Eric Protzer
Paul Summerville

polity

First published in 2022 by Polity Press

Polity Press
65 Bridge Street
Cambridge CB2 1UR, UK

Polity Press
101 Station Landing
Suite 300
Medford, MA 02155, USA

ISBN-13: 978-1-5095-4811-8
ISBN-13: 978-1-5095-4812-5 (pb)

A catalogue record for this book is available from the British Library.

Library of Congress Cataloging-in-Publication Data
Names: Protzer, Eric, author. | Summerville, Paul, author.
Title: Reclaiming populism : how economic fairness can win back disenchanted voters / Eric Protzer, Paul Summerville.
Description: Cambridge ; Medford, MA : Polity, 2021. | Includes bibliographical references and index. | Summary: "Why unfairness, not inequality, is driving the populist upsurge, and what to do about it"-- Provided by publisher.
Identifiers: LCCN 2021016430 (print) | LCCN 2021016431 (ebook) | ISBN 9781509548118 (hardback) | ISBN 9781509548125 (paperback) | ISBN 9781509548132 (epub) | ISBN 9781509550364 (pdf)
Subjects: LCSH: Income distribution--Political aspects--United States. | Populism--United States. | United States--Economic conditions--21st century. | United States--Politics and government--2009-2017. | United States--Politics and government--2017-
Classification: LCC HC106.84 .P77 2021 (print) | LCC HC106.84 (ebook) | DDC 320.56/620973--dc23
LC record available at https://lccn.loc.gov/2021016430
LC ebook record available at https://lccn.loc.gov/2021016431

Typeset in 11 on 13 pt Sabon
by Cheshire Typesetting Ltd, Cuddington, Cheshire
Printed and bound in Great Britain by CPI Group (UK) Ltd, Croydon

For further information on Polity, visit our website:
politybooks.com

Contents

Foreword   vi
Acknowledgments   ix

1 The Inequality Delusion and Other
   Scapegoats for Populism   1

2 The Fairness Instinct   38

3 Economic Unfairness and the Rise of
   Populism   71

4 The Twin Virtues of Equal Opportunity and
   Fair Unequal Outcomes   95

5 Constraints and Solutions to Economic
   Fairness   137

   Conclusion: Scripting a Path Forward   188

References   193
Index   208

Foreword

Enthusiasm for illiberal populist ideas is at fever pitch in nations like the United States and the United Kingdom, and democracy is under threat in a host of other developed countries. Never has it been more important for liberal thinkers from the political mainstream to correctly diagnose what drives this generational challenge and devise corresponding policy prescriptions. With that goal in mind, *Reclaiming Populism* argues that vulnerability to the most severe forms of populism observed in the rich world today can be explained by economic unfairness, where citizens do not get the opportunities and outcomes they believe they deserve. The book then offers concrete direction on how policymakers can identify and rectify sources of economic unfairness in their respective countries, whether they wish to guard against illiberal politics or simply make the lives of their citizens more just.

Crucially, our thesis strongly departs from conventional economic explanations for contemporary rich-world populism. The typical arguments suggest that economic loss or income inequality help to explain the populist backlash. We contend instead that populism is a consequence of more sophisticated forms of economic injustice. *Reclaiming Populism* holds that it matters both why individual citizens get the economic outcomes they do and whether those outcomes are fairly deserved. From this perspective, an economy is fair when each citizen has a real chance at success and when rewards are approximately meritocratic. We make this case not only by referencing existing academic research, but also by showing that low social mobility – an important type of economic unfairness, in which citizens' earnings are deeply influenced by how wealthy their parents were – correlates with indicators of mass support for populism in a variety of settings.

Reclaiming Populism is divided into five chapters. The book exposes the most prominent theories for populism as insufficient or plainly wrong; details why biological and cultural evolution has led citizens across the developed world to especially value fairness; shows how economic unfairness is the necessary condition for contemporary populism in high-income countries; presents a framework of equal opportunity and fair unequal outcomes as policy inputs to economic fairness; and, finally, proposes a diagnostic process to identify binding constraints to economic fairness based on methodology originally developed by Harvard University's Growth Lab.

We received vital help and feedback from many colleagues and friends. We want to thank three in particular. Ron Rogowski gave especially helpful insight on our quantitative work linking social mobility to populism, and on the broad organization of the book's ideas. Rod Tiffen suggested that we specify *fair* unequal outcomes as a category of vital policy inputs in order to differentiate them from inequality which arises from cheating or rent seeking, an innovation that permits a cleaner discussion of the idea of fairness. Our editor George Owers from Polity suggested, among other important things, that our original working title "Defeating Populism" was imprecise because we argue that populism stems from genuine grievances over economic unfairness. We consequently shifted the book's framing toward the current title, *Reclaiming Populism.*

Our book has been written on the shoulders of many others alive and dead. We are most grateful for their assistance, and are, of course, responsible for any errors or omissions.

Acknowledgments

The authors would like to thank the Harvard Growth Lab and the Peter B. Gustavson School of Business for their support.

Many people had a significant impact on this book's ideas from their most incipient stages. We thank Ron Rogowski, Rod Tiffen, Ricardo Hausmann, David Autor, Elisabeth Reynolds, Jeffry Frieden, Robert Lawrence, Gustave Kenedi, Shane Rimmer, Joel Smith, William Irvine, Barry Olshen, Norman Penner, Jeff Brinen, Ze'ev Mankowitz, Michiel Horn, John Holmes, Jim Laxer, Larry Pratt, David Dewitt, Paul Evans, Johanna Falk, Robert Orr, Kenneth S. Courtis, Kumon Shumpei, Michael Donnelly, Charlie McMillian, John Donald, William MacDonald, Rick Wolfe, Wendy Dobson, Robin Sears, Andrew Shipley, John Soukas, David Butler, Chuck Winograd, Mark Faircloth, Mark Redmond, John Hart, David Wolf, Greg Guichon, Steve Paikin, Anne Baumann, Marcus Fedder, John Drake, Carole James, Evan Leeson, David Merner, David Schneider, Nevin Thompson, Bob Rae, Andrew McLeod, Robert Houdet, Jeff Kucharski, Michael Summerville, Tracy Summerville, and Chongfan Tai.

1

The Inequality Delusion and Other Scapegoats for Populism

The response of my 14-year-old students – half of whom qualify for free school meals – to the Veblen suite [London's most expensive hotel room] was interesting. Almost none saw anything wrong in a society where such inequality persists, or anything wrong in the heads of those who wish to spend their money in this way. The consensus was that anyone who made vast sums of money should have vastly expensive things to spend it on. "If I was Jeff Bezos," said one boy who has every intention of becoming him one day, "I would definitely go there." The only shame from the students' point of view was that their teacher didn't get to try it out.

Lucy Kellaway, "My Night as an Oligarch," *Financial Times* (May 2019)

Recent events have given populism a poor reputation. Many countries, like Italy, Greece, Poland, Hungary, the Czech Republic, and Slovakia, are now caught up in populist eruptions that have moved them away in varying degrees from pluralist democracy, and in some cases, near authoritarian rule. More troubling is the fact that this list also includes countries that have served the world as important beacons of liberal democracy, like the United States, the United Kingdom, and France.

1

The Inequality Delusion and Other Scapegoats

The populist politicians who have captured and shaped this upheaval claim that society is rigged for elites, by elites. They correspondingly advocate various illiberal "solutions." Free and fair elections, the rule of law, freedom of religion, press freedom, free speech, free trade, nondiscriminatory immigration, nonpartisan state bureaucracy, and international institutions have all become targets of the contemporary populist onslaught.

In response, scores of commentators, academics, political leaders, policymakers, and citizens are not just concerned, but *horrified*. Populism, in this view, is an aberration that has no place in liberal democracy and must simply be vanquished. Yet it is important to remember that populism has not always been an obviously bad thing. The term "populism" was first used to describe the People's Party in late nineteenth-century America, which was not only anti-trade and anti-immigration but also, critically, anti-monopoly and anti-corruption. The People's Party fused with the Democratic Party in 1896, and a number of its core proposals ultimately became seminal American economic policy under the New Deal: ending the gold standard, instituting progressive taxation, and regulating anti-competitive business practices. However uncomfortable it may be to accept, the fact is that populist voters have historically protested key societal injustices and often paved the way for much-needed reform.

Liberal democracy is indeed in peril today, but we will argue that this is not because the populist electorate is somehow villainous. Instead, contemporary developed-world populism stems from voters who think that the rules of society are unfairly rigged. These disenchanted citizens have reason to believe that opportunity is not equal, that economic rewards do not match contributions, and that the much-cherished rules of meritocracy

2

are broken. The burden to address this problem in a way that preserves freedom and the rule of law rests, of course, with mainstream politicians. Unfortunately, these leaders have largely met populist grievances with misapprehension and condescension instead of empathy – leaving illiberal actors to fill the vacuum. This disconnect is especially tragic because, properly diagnosed and prescribed, addressing the problem of economic unfairness could turn the illiberal shift now underway into something positive.

Crucially, the problem of economic unfairness as discussed herein is very different from, and in important respects incompatible with, typical ideas about how economic inequality or economic losses could lead to political disruption. In fact, *Reclaiming Populism* contends that modern economic thought has taken a serious wrong turn by analyzing economic injustice almost wholly in such rudimentary terms. In reality, humans do not care simply about whether economic losses, gains, and inequalities occur, but about the underlying reasons *why* they occur – and, accordingly, whether those outcomes are *fairly deserved* by each individual. In this view, it is fundamentally absurd to attempt to explain populism in terms of a society's overall economic inequality, because that calculation does not consider whether the inequality in question results fairly or unfairly from differences between citizens.

The chapters that follow will answer a number of important questions about populism and economic fairness. How should we understand the contemporary populist complaint of unfairness? How has that unfairness led to populism? Why have mainstream political parties failed to credibly tackle the problem of unfairness, leaving it to the radical fringe? What policy prescriptions can be used to address unfairness, and

3

which ones are relevant in any particular country? Is there a script that political leaders who value pluralism can follow to win back disenchanted voters?

This task will be accomplished in three main ways. First, with reference to established academic research. There are good reasons to doubt many of the major extant theories of populism, for instance, and there is much evidence that biological and cultural evolution have led citizens of modern high-income societies to care profoundly about fairness. Second, through original regression analysis. We will show that low social mobility (an important type of economic unfairness, where citizens' economic success is strongly influenced by how wealthy their parents were) consistently correlates with measures of populism across the developed world. While virtually no country is completely free from any populist influence, relatively worse social mobility is systematically associated with relatively higher support for populism. In contrast, many of the "scapegoats" for populism exhibit no such systematic correlation. Third, through a policy-oriented diagnostic framework based on methodology developed by Harvard University's Growth Lab. We will organize key policy inputs to economic fairness under the twin virtues of equal opportunity and fair unequal outcomes; and then explain, with examples, how a policymaker can identify and rectify the binding constraints to economic unfairness in their particular country.

To begin, this chapter critically examines the main existing theories for populism other than economic unfairness. It will show that many are attractive at first glance, but that under scrutiny none can fully explain the populist wave and several are not very credible at all. Together, however, the most useful and robust insights point toward another hypothesis, which the remainder of the book investigates in detail: economic unfairness.

What Makes a Good Theory for Populism?

Prominent theories for populism include immigration, social media, generational value differences, income inequality, international trade shocks, and the Global Financial Crisis (GFC). There are compelling anecdotal arguments for each, but in order to *systematically* understand which ideas are most useful to explain populism we need a framework to assess them. Three criteria are arguably important. First, hypotheses for populism must be theoretically plausible. One should be able to imagine why the supposed root cause is problematic, and how it could lead to populism specifically. Second, theories ought to match the geography of developed-world populism. While illiberal populism is threatening, it is conspicuously *not* all-encompassing across every rich country. Third, the timeline of the theory should match that of the contemporary populist wave from its early bloom to full flowering. A useful theory must, in sum, address the *why*, the *where*, and the *when* of populism.

Applying the first of these criteria requires some comprehension of the key characteristics of populism. While there is no universally accepted definition of populism, several good ones exist and they generally have common features. Müller (2016) describes populism as a form of political expression that sets a supposedly unified people against elites who are somehow corrupt or morally inferior. Populist leaders also claim exclusive representation of the "true people," to the point that opposing candidates are inherently illegitimate. Thus populism, to Müller's mind, is an essentially anti-elite and anti-pluralist type of identity politics. Norris and Inglehart (2019) emphasize the anti-elite and identitarian aspects of populism, but also contend that populism is a specifically authoritarian style of governance. Eichengreen (2018) largely agrees with Norris and Inglehart's definition.

Guriev and Papaioannou (2020) review the relevant academic literature, and observe that most modern definitions characterize populism as *anti-elite* and *anti-pluralist*. Different authors then variously argue for additional qualities such as authoritarianism, short-termism, and nativism. For our purposes, we will rely on the two essential qualities of anti-elitism and anti-pluralism, which capture the main thrust of today's populist politics. Anti-elitism, for one, depicts society as an unlevel playing field rigged against the "real" people to benefit an immoral elite. This does not mean that populism is spiteful about every powerful individual, as Donald Trump overwhelmingly proved. Populism is specifically suspicious of those elites who are perceived to get ahead by cheating others. In part this leads to the populist view that good leadership is down to personal identity – that it's important to have the *right* kinds of elites in power, who purportedly ally themselves with the "true" people.

This nuance informs the second key characteristic of populism: anti-pluralism, or the claim that all opponents of the populist leadership are inherently illegitimate. If good leadership is thought to be a function of personal identity rather than institutional constraints or democratic legitimacy, populist voters may insist that their candidate *alone* is qualified to govern. The consequences of anti-pluralism can range from conspiratorial claims of election-rigging to calls to incarcerate political opponents.

These two characteristics of populism, anti-elitism and anti-pluralism, also help establish what it is not. First, populism is not characterized by a left- or right-wing political orientation. Although right-wing populists such as Trump (in the US) and Marine Le Pen (in France) may be somewhat more common in the developed world today, there are also left-wing populist movements like Greece's Syriza that are just as anti-elite and anti-pluralist. Left- and right-wing populists simply offer different policy prescriptions to address similar underlying anger. Second, populism is not automatically interchangeable with political extremism of any sort. Twentieth-century fascism was frequently pro-elite, for instance, and Jeremy Corbyn's platform for the 2019 UK general election was largely thought to be hard left but certainly not anti-pluralist.

An important but overlooked nuance of theories for why populism occurs is whether it results from changes in political demand or supply. The bulk of the academic and popular discussion around populism concentrates on demand-side factors, or causes which have led to changes in voter preferences. But it is also conceivable that there could be supply-side effects, where political parties change their platforms in response to some event regardless of voter preferences. For example, one could theorize that political parties could deliberately take more extreme cultural positions after an unexpected migration inflow to inflame and excite the electorate. Although this book will primarily concentrate on demand-side theories, it is important to bear in mind the possibility of this alternative channel.

Next let us examine *where* the populist wave has most forcefully taken root. The focus of our concern is on high-income countries with advanced democratic institutions. To be sure, there are populists in the developing world, for example Jair Bolsonaro in Brazil and Rodrigo Duterte in the Philippines. But this pattern is not especially surprising. Many developing countries have long histories of fragile democracy and troubled demagoguery. What is so unsettling about the current wave of populism is that it is even affecting countries that were long considered to be core examples of liberal pluralist democracy.

It is very important to understand that populism, insofar as it occurs within this particular scope, is *not* a binary outcome. It differs substantially by degree, and there is a crucial difference between countries where populism explodes the status quo and those that keep support for populism within manageable levels. On the one hand, Brexit and the populist forces behind it have thoroughly upended British politics and institutions, and will undoubtedly be remembered as a major disruption to its democracy. The Trump phenomenon has likewise massively altered American politics, economic policy, international relations, and more. In contrast, the Netherlands has experienced non-negligible electoral support for populist parties like the Party for Freedom, but this has not led to the same level of upheaval. Some of that electoral success, in fact, undoubtedly derives from the Netherlands' proportional representation election system, which gives even small political groups a voice in parliament. Several Nordic countries have also experienced material levels of populism, especially in the wake of the 2015 European migrant crisis; but, as Chapter 3 will discuss, this arguably led to a reassessment of multiculturalism rather than to any substantial abandonment of the liberal democratic status quo. Support for populism is tangible in these latter cases, but it has neither imperiled democracy nor seriously disrupted institutions.

The nonbinary nature of populism makes it difficult to analyze through qualitative, anecdotal comparisons alone. How can you appropriately judge the strength of populism in a way that is valid across different settings? When is a chosen comparator either valid or invalid vis-à-vis another? Because of issues like these, this book will chiefly approach the question of where populism has taken hold, and to what extent, through quantitative analysis. Even more specifically, we set out to exclusively examine quantifiable measures of populism that are directly comparable across each comparator, and eschew measures which may have different interpretations in different settings. In Protzer (2019), a technical companion to this book that is available online, we accordingly perform multiple regression analysis to investigate correlates of the geography of populism in four settings.

First, we examine support for Trump in the 2016 and 2020 US presidential elections. We specifically look at the county-level vote *swing* in the Republican presidential vote share from 2012 to the year in question; Trump was an insurgent within his own party, and thus support for populism cannot be readily inferred from the raw Republican vote share. This is a standard approach in the academic literature, used, for example, by Broz et al. (2019).

Second, we examine the department-level vote share for Le Pen in the second round of the 2017 French presidential election. In contrast to Trump, Le Pen was not an insurgent in her own party and thus the raw vote *share* rather than the vote *swing* best reflects populist voting preferences.

Third, we analyze the national vote share for populist parties in the 2019 European Parliament election. We use the *PopuList* classification of populist European parties from Rooduijn et al. (2019) to tabulate each country's vote share for populist and far-right parties (the latter of which we use to cast a wider net that includes, for example, Greece's Golden Dawn), and, in a robustness check, we examine purely populist parties. Although European Parliament elections are stereotypically considered unimportant by European Union (EU) citizens, the 2019 election had an unprecedentedly high turnout rate of 51 percent – comparable to levels in American presidential elections. European Parliament elections are also advantageous to consider because they are perhaps the only valid example of cross-national elections where citizens of different countries vote under the same rules.

Fourth, we consider the World Gallup Poll's surveyed confidence in national government across different developed countries (averaged for each country over 2015 to 2019 to capture the key years in the eruption of modern populism) as a proxy for populist political discontent with the status quo. This measure has previously been used by Aksoy et al. (2018) in the context of international support for populism. Although it is an indirect proxy, its uniformity makes for valid cross-national comparisons.

For the reasons touched on above, we refrain from simply comparing electoral results from separate elections in our quantitative analysis. Vote shares cannot readily be compared across different electoral systems, and thus will not yield valid indicators of relative support for populism. For instance, the first-past-the-post system used in countries that follow the Westminster Model strongly discourages voting for small parties, whereas proportional representation tends not to penalize voting for political parties based on size.

In its totality, the quantitative analysis considers at various points countries that either belong to the EU or have GDP per capita levels of at least $25,000. Perfect data coverage for all our variables of interest (especially social mobility) is never fully available, and we discard severe outliers as needed, but in each setting we manage to examine a consistent and substantial portion of potentially relevant comparators. In the US, we consider 2,750 out of 3,143 counties; in France, we consider 39 of the largest metropolitan departments out of 96, which together cover more than 60 percent of the French population; in the EU, we consider 19 of 28 of its 2019 members, which in general are its largest and wealthiest;[1] and in the context of national confidence in government from 2015 to 2019, we consider 24 developed countries.[2] In robustness checks for the last two settings we selectively examine wealthier countries to ensure our results are not sensitive to these definitions of what it means to be "developed." Importantly, the international analyses allow us to examine not just classically Western but also East European countries, including Croatia, the Czech Republic, Romania, Slovakia, and Slovenia, in addition to Japan.

Although this book relies on the quantitative correlations established in Protzer (2019), it complements them with qualitative discussion. As noted, such comparisons are not as precise as their quantitative counterparts. But they are essential to flesh out the theoretical reasons why certain countries have experienced pronounced support for illiberal populism. Why, for instance, has the US been so severely disrupted by Trump (a deep threat still, given Joe Biden's razor-thin 2020 victory and Trump's

[1] Austria, Belgium, Croatia, the Czech Republic, Denmark, Finland, France, Germany, Greece, Ireland, Italy, Luxembourg, the Netherlands, Portugal, Romania, Slovakia, Spain, Sweden, and the UK.

[2] Australia, Austria, Belgium, Canada, the Czech Republic, Denmark, Finland, France, Germany, Ireland, Italy, Japan, Luxembourg, the Netherlands, New Zealand, Norway, Portugal, Slovakia, Slovenia, Spain, Sweden, Switzerland, the UK, and the US.

hold over the Republican Party) when populism has not gathered steam in Australia, Canada, or New Zealand? When most European countries have managed to keep the thrust of populism at manageable levels, why has the UK been so thoroughly derailed by the populist forces behind Brexit? Why did a third of the French citizenry back Le Pen in both presidential and EU Parliament elections, and more than 70 percent claim to support the populist, massively disruptive Gilets Jaunes (Yellow Vests) movement? Why is Italian politics dominated by the populist Northern League and Five-Star Movement, which have at various points advocated for Italy's exit from the EU, northern Italy's secession from the rest of the country, and the implementation of direct democracy?

Finally, we need to trace out the timeline of the current populist wave, the *when*. In particular, it is important to overcome a common misperception that populism has been a "bolt from the blue" – that a series of political earthquakes simply started appearing from roughly 2015 onwards. It's vital to understand that such severe discontent cannot easily be flipped on like a light switch, but more plausibly builds up over a considerable period of time.

There is much evidence that anti-establishment political anger has been growing over several decades. Colantone and Stanig (2018b) show that the far-right vote share in Europe has been increasing steadily since the 1980s. Golder (2016) draws the same conclusion. Figures 1.1–3 showcase relevant trends in the US, the UK, and France. Figure 1.1 demonstrates that political polarization has been rising in the US since the 1990s, captured by measuring how much Republicans and Democrats diverge on whether they hold conservative values. These increasingly different and extreme values

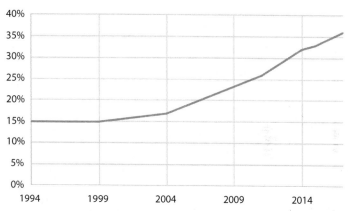

Figure 1.1: USA – Gap in the share taking a conservative position by major party affiliation

Source: Pew Research Center 2017

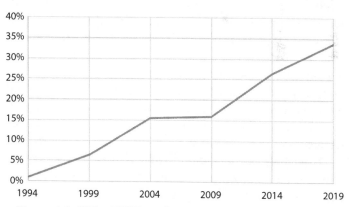

Figure 1.2: UK – UKIP and Brexit Party vote share in EU Parliament elections

set the stage for the "us versus them" mentality of populist leaders. Figure 1.2 shows that Brexit shouldn't have been surprising, as the Leave campaign was based on a political movement that had been growing since the 1990s. Finally, Figure 1.3 shows that the National

Figure 1.3: France – National Front/Rally vote share in first round of presidential elections

Rally has been an important force in French politics since the 1980s. We should accordingly prize explanations for populism that are compatible with this longer timeframe.

The contemporary wave of populism across the developed world arose as a collection of anti-elite and anti-pluralist political movements; it has taken hold in certain countries, and certain parts of countries, but not across the entire developed world; and it has grown over the past few decades, particularly since the 1980s. Any good theory for populism must therefore be able to explain why this defined political outcome has occurred in addition to its geography and timeline.

The Conventional Explanations for Populism

Theories that attempt to explain contemporary populism in the developed world are generally divided into two schools: cultural and economic. The former contends that unprecedented social change has created conditions for rising intolerance and anxiety. The latter argues that globalization and technological change have generated far-reaching economic insecurity and inequity. These two approaches are, of course, not mutually exclusive. It is, in principle at least, possible that some combination of these factors has led to populism.

Three cultural and three economic theories for populism are especially prominent. In the first category are immigration, social media, and intergenerational value differences. In the second are income and wealth inequality, shocks from global trade, and the fallout of the GFC. This section looks first at arguments and evidence for each of these theories in turn. The following section will then critically examine them in terms of the three criteria stated above: the *why*, the *where*, and the *when* of populism. As we will show, most of these arguments actually offer little insight. Some, however, although by themselves incomplete, are illuminating and hint at populism's deeper cause.

First, populism has been blamed on excessive immigration. Kaufmann (2018) advances this idea, and numerous academic studies tie exogenous immigration shocks to populism and support for the far right: Becker and Fetzer (2016) in the case of the UK, Barone et al. (2016) for Italy, Edo et al. (2019) for France, and Halla et al. (2017) for Austria. Mutz (2018) makes a comparable argument for the US, linking surveyed feelings of status threat among white Americans to the 2016 vote for Trump. Altogether, unprecedented levels of immigration have become a convenient explanation for economic, political, social, and cultural dislocation. Populists like Le Pen, Kristian Thulesen Dahl (in Denmark), and Nigel Farage (in the UK) are widely recognized for capitalizing on these perceived disruptions through xenophobic electoral platforms. In some nations, such as the Nordic countries, even mainstream parties have arguably been pressured to adopt stronger stances against multiculturalism and open borders as a result of broader anti-immigrant sentiment.

In the case of the US, the composition of migrants has shifted away from Europe and toward Latin America and Asia, although migration flows as a proportion of the population are lower than historical highs. Notwithstanding the long history of anti-Irish, anti-Italian, anti-Semitic, and anti-Eastern European backlashes, the rise of visible minority immigrants has co-occurred with the rise of populism and is purported to explain it. Illegal immigration, namely from Mexico and Central America, has especially added fuel to the fire. By 2015, the percentage of foreign-born people living in the United States had tripled since the 1970s, from 4.7 percent to 13.4 percent. The UK experienced a similar transition in the composition of its population. In 1960 around 3 percent of the British population was foreign-born; the figure is now closer to 14 percent. In particular, Eastern European migration, principally from Poland, exacerbated complaints about immigration in the UK after 2004.

There is much evidence that many citizens genuinely feel threatened by immigration. For example, in the US a majority of Republicans now believe that the white race faces discrimination in America, and that too much openness to immigration risks the loss of national identity. Similar concerns echo across Western Europe, especially since the 2015 migrant crisis.

Second, populism is blamed on the rise of social media driving political polarization through fake news and echo chambers. Sunstein (2018) explores this phenomenon, while Guriev et al. (2019) show that access to 3G mobile network coverage is associated with lower confidence in government. It is well known that the internet can fuel leveraged, narrow perspectives that result in groupthink and misinformation, and help to breed extreme views. Social media platforms like Facebook and Twitter have access to mammoth volumes of highly personal data that can predict your personality more accurately than your spouse or parents can. An especially dangerous but effective tactic is to sort people into groups of like-minded political, social, and cultural tribes that rally against a supposed common enemy. That process is deeply rooted in our evolutionary tribal history, where emotional arousal to fight and kill an outside enemy contributed to the survival of early communities.

Social media has been blamed for both the rise of a far right that hates foreigners and uses fascist symbols, and an illiberal far left that demands recognition for minorities but demonizes the "privileged." Both cases can be explained as forms of identity politics, where an in-group is revered and an out-group detested. These movements are made even more influential given their networked nature. For example, fierce nationalist movements now support each other cross-nationally. It also inspires people who have never met to commit violence against perceived common enemies, as the October 2020 murder of Parisian teacher Samuel Paty tragically demonstrated.

Third, populism has been attributed to clashing values held by older and younger generations, importantly by Norris and Inglehart (2019). As they note elsewhere, the modern world has produced a generation of young adults with globalist values and, consequently, a "growing generational gap . . . is likely to heighten the salience of cultural cleavage in party politics . . . irrespective of any improvements in the underlying economic conditions" (2016: 31). There tends to be more support among younger people for environmental protection, cultural diversity, and LGBT rights. Notably, the expression of these values is sometimes intolerant of disagreeing perspectives. Norris and Inglehart explain that older generations "resent being told that traditional values are 'politically incorrect'" and that "they have come to feel that they are being marginalized within their own countries" (2016: 29). Thus populist leaders have argued for the need to protect traditional values and staunch the flow of people before those values are permanently displaced.

Fourth, what Norris and Inglehart identify as "perhaps the most widely-held view of mass support for populism – the *economic inequality* perspective" – is that too much wealth has gone to too few people (2016: 2). This argument purports that wealth and income inequality are central to the rise of populism in certain market democracies, and that the simple prescription is radical redistribution. The degree to which developed-world income inequality has risen in recent decades is certainly alarming and well publicized. Some key facts in the US include that the proportion of national income received by the top 1 percent has doubled since the 1970s; college-educated workers earn at least 30 percent more (in real terms) than they did in the 1960s, yet high-school graduates have seen pay gains of only 10 percent; and CEOs made roughly 20 times what an average employee did in the 1960s, whereas today that ratio has risen to around 300.

The growth of income and wealth inequality would appear to be an obvious source of today's raging economic, political, social, and cultural anger. Major thought leaders – including several Nobel Laureates in economics – have, accordingly, sounded the alarm on unequal outcomes in all its forms, depicting it alone as the paramount disease that is destroying the democratic social contract. Among many, consider Joseph Stiglitz's *The Price of Inequality* (2012), Thomas Piketty's seminal *Capital in the Twenty-First Century* (2014), or even some of Paul Krugman's columns in the *New York Times*. This line of thought specifically contends that unequal economic outcomes have caused populism because people do not like living in highly unequal societies.

A more sophisticated version of this argument presents populism as the result of inequality-driven institutional decay – Nolan (2017), for example, touches on this perspective. It often begins by drawing on Piketty's *Capital in the Twenty-First Century*, which argues that wealth inequality tends to rise over time because rates of return to capital typically exceed rates of overall GDP growth. Scheidel (2018) makes a similar argument grounded in history rather than economics – that inequality inevitably increases over time and is only disrupted by plagues, famines, mass migration, or mass warfare. Having established that growing inequality has been an essential feature of capitalism, Daron Acemoglu's line of institutional research demonstrates why sharply unequal outcomes are bad for democracy – see, for example, Acemoglu and Robinson (2012). The responsible mechanism is that economic inequality concentrates de facto power among a narrow elite, who then wield it to reshape de jure political and economic institutions in their favor.

Fifth, a well-regarded academic argument is that populism can be explained by the negative impacts of trade shocks on labor markets. There is good evidence that trade with China has systematically undermined job security in the US (Autor et al. 2016). By embracing the investment, trade, and employment consequences of breakneck globalization, it is argued, US employees came to be replaced by Chinese counterparts who can perform the same tasks at a lower cost. Rodrik (2018: 19) explains how deeply frustrating the negative employment consequences of trade shocks can be: "it's one thing to lose your job to someone who competes under the same rules as you do. It's a different thing when you lose your job to someone who takes advantage of lax labor, environmental, tax, or safety standards in other countries." There is convincing research which links these sorts of job losses to the rise of populism in the US (Autor et al. 2020) and in the UK (Colantone and Stanig 2016).

Like most other categories of explanations for populism, the bulk of ideas associated with globalization are on the political demand side – they examine how trade shocks could lead to changes in voters' preferences. Rodrik (2020), however, highlights two ways in which globalization-associated shocks could induce populism through the political supply side. One possibility is that trade shocks inherently lead politicians to adopt more extreme and differentiated positions on whether to enact populist trade protections, so as to take advantage of the "hot issue" of the day. Another possibility is that globalization-related shocks could make it harder for right-wing parties to compete on laissez-faire economic principles, so they deliberately inflame populist cultural issues as an alternative path to victory. There is scant empirical evidence on these understudied ideas, but they are worth bearing in mind as potentially plausible.

Finally, some argue that the 2008–9 GFC was responsible for the rise of populism. Interestingly, Funke et al. (2016) show that financial crises, on average, resulted in 30 percent more support for far-right parties among high-income countries from 1870 to 2014. The authors show that the GFC repeated this pattern, and may therefore explain some part of the political outrage behind populism. Tooze (2018) delves into the links between the global financial crisis and the rise of populism in depth. There were painful immediate results of the GFC which substantiate this relationship, like mass foreclosure. But the prolonged aftermath of the financial crisis has been, in some ways, just as painful. Historically low "emergency" interest rates have made owners of capital – the real beneficiaries of loose monetary policy – far richer. At the same time, the fiscal austerity imposed in many high-income countries, a consequence of the crisis, marginalized the disenfranchised poor and struggling middle class.

Scapegoats and Deeper Causes for Populism

Individually or together, these theories are attractive explanations for the present-day populist challenges faced by some market democracies. The evidence is that many citizens do feel disenfranchised – economically, politically, socially, and culturally. As we will demonstrate, however, none, alone or together, can account for the populist wave, and they do not fully explain the deeper mechanism at work. We will now examine these theories using the framework outlined at the beginning of the chapter – the *why*, the *where*, and the *when* of the populist wave.

First, consider the family of cultural arguments: immigration, social media, and intergenerational value differences. Any analysis of how these variables may or may not explain contemporary developed-world populism must begin with the caveat that, of course, culture *always* matters in politics. While the simultaneous onset of populism across much of the developed world suggests a common cause, its unfolding is, at the very least, tempered by country-specific characteristics. For example, Trumpian populism is deeply influenced by America's tortured history of race relations; his promised border wall was founded on longstanding racist perceptions of Hispanics, and his "Muslim ban" on entry to the US was partly a consequence of America's trauma surrounding 9/11. In France, comparably, the National Rally (Rassemblement national; until 2018 known as the National Front) aims to specifically combat the influence of Islam, which is, in part, due to the country's colonial legacy and its experience with domestic terrorism. Policymakers must recognize cultural realities in order to design an effective response to populism.

Nevertheless, immigration, social media, and intergenerational value differences do not seem plausible as *exogenous*, independent causes of populism. This is mainly because, as we demonstrate in Protzer (2019), they are incompatible with the *where* of populism. This is evident, to begin with, in the lack of a consistent correlation between the geography of populism and immigration levels. After taking control variables into account, there is a statistically significant *negative* correlation between the share of immigrants in a US county and the vote swing toward Trump in 2016 versus 2012; whereas the 2020 vote swing toward Trump versus that of 2012 has a marginally significant positive correlation with the share of immigrants in a county's population. At the same time, there is no statistically significant correlation between the fraction of births to immigrant parents and the vote share for Le Pen in the second round of the 2017 French presidential election; nor between the share of immigrants in the population and confidence in government across different developed countries; and nor between the share of immigrants in the population and the fraction of votes for populist and far-right parties by country in the 2019 European Parliament election. As a robustness check, we also examine the *change* in the share of immigrants in the population from 2000 to 2015 in the context of the 2019 European Parliament election (a potentially relevant indicator in this case, due to perceptions of rising immigration resulting from new EU accessions) and find that it is likewise statistically insignificant. On the whole, there is not, therefore, a persuasive positive correlation between the geography of immigration and developed-world populism.

Although a number of previously mentioned studies tie immigration to populism, the literature comes with some important caveats which shed doubt on that relationship. For one, too many studies – such as Kaufmann (2018) and Mutz (2018) – draw the flawed conclusion that immigration causes populism based on survey results, where individual populist voters often report hostility to immigrants. The core problem with this approach is that it simply argues that citizens vote for populists because they have populist attitudes, which nearly amounts to a truism. Such survey-based methodologies typically do not investigate the exogenous causal origins of *why* citizens hold those values to begin with, which may in fact have nothing to do with immigration whatsoever. Academics call this the "attitudes on attitudes" problem; as Colantone and Stanig (2018a: 4) explain, "attitudes should be considered 'bad controls' . . . in regressions aimed at investigating the impact of economic conditions on voting. In fact, changes in attitudes are themselves an important channel through which economic variables might affect voting."

Other studies take a more methodologically sound approach by examining how exogenous immigration shocks affect voting patterns, rather than relying solely on surveys of voters' attitudes. Nevertheless, the empirical results are mixed. In addition to the previously mentioned work, which finds positive associations between immigration and populism, Colantone and Stanig (2016) show that immigrant stocks were *negatively* associated with the Leave vote in the UK Brexit referendum; and Vertier and Viskanic (2018) find that French municipalities become *less* populist after receiving refugees.

Moreover, there is a bigger picture that many single-country studies miss: plenty of Western nations with large foreign-born populations do not face the same populist challenge. For instance, much is made of the immigration acceleration in the UK in the 2000s and the rise of the UK Independence Party (UKIP). The share of foreign-born residents in Britain rose from below 8 percent in the 1990s to nearly 14 percent in the 2010s, in part due to new EU accessions in Eastern Europe, and by 2015 and 2016 immigration frequently polled as the top election issue. Similar concerns abound in France and Italy, whose populations are now, respectively, approximately 13 percent and 10 percent foreign-born. All three of these countries, Britain, France, and Italy, have experienced serious populist upheaval, evident in the fact that their electorates voted for populists at whopping rates in the range of 30–50 percent in the 2019 European Parliament election. Yet, at the same time, the Netherlands, Denmark, and Ireland have similar immigrant stocks – at 13 percent, 13 percent, and 17 percent of the population, respectively – but had far lower populist vote shares of 7 percent, 11 percent, and 12 percent, respectively, in the same election. The contrast among new world countries is even starker. If immigration is truly an exogenous cause of populism, it is puzzling that the US, where 15 percent of the population is foreign-born, elected Trump, but that Canada, New Zealand, and Australia – where those numbers are, respectively, 21 percent, 22 percent, and 30 percent – have not been susceptible to populism.

Neither can one identify populist versus nonpopulist countries by their refugee stocks, which one might suppose to be more politically salient. In 2015, 0.08 percent of people in the US were refugees as opposed to 0.42 percent in Canada and 0.15 percent in Australia. The UK, France, and Italy hosted refugees accounting for 0.18 percent, 0.41 percent, and 0.16 percent of their populations, versus 0.32 percent for Denmark and 0.91 percent for Norway.

These facts make it very difficult to conclude that high levels of immigration *systematically* lead to populism. If this were true, we would expect larger populist explosions in Canada rather than the US, and in Ireland rather than Britain. On balance, it is more likely that disdain for foreigners results from whatever malaise leads to populism, and that immigration shocks *amplify* the problem in susceptible countries. A telling series of interviews about German populism by *The Economist* (2019c) found that "many easterners resented the resources being devoted to help newcomers when they felt left behind. They also disliked the labelling of their complaints as racist." Recall that Trump was elected in considerable part because he won over individuals from key swing states who previously had voted for Barack Obama, and are therefore unlikely to be hard-core racists. In fact, Grimmer and Marble (2019) show that the average voter for Mitt Romney in 2012 was more racist than the average Trump voter in 2016. The attraction of Trump's nationalism plausibly has more to do with status and economic anxiety than with racial hatred, as argued by Fukuyama (2018). This trend was perhaps even more evident in the 2020 US presidential election, as Trump gained support relative to 2016 among African American and Hispanic voters.

There is a similar disconnect between the geography of social media uptake and populism. Although granular subnational data is generally not available, national rates of active social media use are not statistically significantly related to either populist and far-right vote shares in the 2019 European Parliament election or confidence in national government. While approximately 60 percent of people in the US and UK actively use social media, that is also true of nonpopulist Australia, Canada, and Portugal. Social media penetration rates in France and Italy are even lower, at around 50 percent. Conversely, two-thirds of people in Norway and Denmark use social media, as do 70 percent of New Zealanders and a whopping three-quarters of South Koreans. If social media is an exogenous cause of populism, New Zealand and South Korea should have been among its primary casualties.

The timeline of populism also poses a challenge for theories about social media. Much speculation about the role of social media in the rise of populism centers on the misperception that both are very recent phenomena. But, as explained, populism in fact originated more than thirty-five years ago. Facebook, conversely, was only founded in 2004; it took until 2008 for it to hit 100 million global users, and until 2012 for it to gain 1 billion global users. Something else must be at work.

What's more, there is some evidence that the direct connection between social media and populism is dubious. Groshek and Koc-Michalska (2017) find that active social media use actually decreased support for the Republican Party in the 2016 US presidential election, while passive and uncivil use of social media had an effect similar to that of conventional daytime television. In totality, social media is, like immigration, most plausibly a potential *amplifier* of populism rather than a root cause.

The argument that generational value differences explain populism is, as indicated, foremostly championed by Norris and Inglehart. They convincingly show that citizens who vote for populists tend to have morally conservative, authoritarian values, and are generally older. While this contributes a great deal toward describing populist outcomes, however, it does not fully explain *why* those outcomes occur. To understand why the older voters in question have come to hold populist authoritarian values requires some additional exogenous cause.

An obvious possibility to consider, in line with this same argument, is that citizens vote for populists because they belong to older generations that reject the typically liberal, globalist values of many of today's youth. But it is not true that older societies are systematically more populist. The share of seniors in the population was statistically significantly correlated with the vote swing toward Trump in 2016 and 2020 versus 2012, but there was no such correlation with the populist and far-right vote share in the 2019 European Parliament election, nor with confidence in national government among different countries. Indeed, the five nations with the highest shares of seniors in the population – at rates all above 20 percent – are Japan, Italy, Germany, Portugal, and Finland. Among these, only Italy is strongly populist, Germany and Finland are somewhat mixed cases, and Japan and Portugal are conspicuously resistant to populism.

On the whole, the generational value differences argument suffers from an "attitudes on attitudes" problem, like some of the immigration studies noted previously: it uses populist attitudes to explain populist voting patterns, which are themselves an indicator of attitudes. To be sure, studies like that of Norris and Inglehart provide useful and insightful descriptions – people who vote for populists tend to hold certain values, and it is important to understand what those values are. But some other hypothesis, for example trade shocks or income inequality, is needed to adequately explain why those attitudes exist to begin with.

Although these cultural variables – immigration, social media, and the presence of older generations – thus cannot serve as systematic exogenous explanations for the illiberal populist threat, that does not mean cultural issues are irrelevant. Policymakers should simply understand these problems as symptoms and amplifiers. Addressing them might help manage populism – but is unlikely to remove the fundamental threat.

Next, consider the three major economic theories for the rise of populism: inequality of income and wealth, trade shocks from globalization, and the fallout of the GFC. As noted, the first of these explanations is especially prominent in both popular and academic discourse. But as it turns out, the income inequality hypothesis is also the *least* credible of any assessed in this book.

To begin with, the empirical relationship between inequalities of income and wealth versus patterns of global populism is not convincing. In Protzer (2019) we show that county-level income inequality had a statistically significant *negative* correlation with the vote swing toward Trump in both 2016 and 2020 versus 2012. While the correlation between a French department's income inequality and its vote share for Le Pen was positive and significant, there was no statistically significant correlation in the cases of either the 2019 European Parliament election or confidence in national government. Wealth inequality also was significantly *positively* correlated with confidence in government. Similarly, it was marginally significantly *negatively* correlated with votes for populists and the far right in the 2019 European Parliament election. Thus there is no robust positive relationship between income and wealth inequality, and the geography of contemporary developed-world populism.

Intuitively, one might consider how income inequality in France and Italy is fairly low by developed-world standards, whereas the US is renowned for its exceptionally high income inequality, and yet all three countries are beset by fierce populist movements. At the same time, according to the OECD, strongly populism-resistant countries like Australia and Portugal have higher levels of income inequality than Italy and, especially, France. In fact, the weak statistical connection between unequal outcomes and populism has already been noted by prominent academics. Rodrik (2019) notes that "conventional indicators of inequality are a poor predictor of economic and political discontent in democracies."

An equally important reason to reject the inequality hypothesis is that it is theoretically weak. The key argument linking inequality to populism contends that people dislike unequal outcomes, and populism is the political manifestation of that problem. However, the claim that humans are systematically averse to unequal outcomes is in fact a delusion. This intuition is wonderfully captured by the conclusion drawn by *Financial Times* columnist turned working-class math teacher, Lucy Kellaway, that among her lower-income students, "[a]lmost none saw anything wrong in a society where

... inequality persists, or anything wrong in the heads of those who wish to spend their money in this way." Yale psychologists Starmans et al. (2017) offer a systematic view of the matter: they analyze a wide range of behavioral studies on unequal economic outcomes and conclude that "there is no evidence that people are bothered by economic inequality itself. Rather, they are bothered by something that is often confounded with inequality: economic unfairness." In reality, some unequal outcomes are fairly produced (e.g., someone works hard, innovates, or uses innate talents) and some are unfairly produced (e.g., someone steals or gets ahead through nepotism). On the whole, people strongly prefer *fair* economic outcomes, where rewards correspond to contribution, regardless of whether they are equal or not.

The central importance of *fair* rather than *equal* economic outcomes is a major theme of this book that later chapters will explore in detail. For the moment, however, one might consider a stylized example to help build intuition: the popular negativity toward billionaires that is often chalked up to inequality aversion is not as simple as might first appear, and can be understood better through the lens of fairness. As *The Economist* (2019b) noted, Swedes hold far more positive attitudes toward billionaires than Americans do. Could this be because Swedish billionaires contribute less to inequality than their American counterparts? Actually, the opposite is true: Swedish billionaires hold wealth amounting to a quarter of the country's GDP, one of the highest rates in the world. But critically, Swedish billionaires have obtained their wealth through considerably less rent-seeking than American billionaires. Rent-seeking amounts to accruing wealth through channels like monopoly power and lobbying rather than productivity, and notoriously distorts competition. This suggests that perceptions of billionaires depend not on how unequal their outcomes are, but on whether those outcomes were achieved in a fair way. *The Economist* explained that "the popularity of billionaires [in Sweden] is partly owing to the perception that they have made their money not by exploiting ordinary Swedes, but by creating multinationals such as H&M, Volvo and Spotify."

Of course, the sorry history of communism also overwhelmingly demonstrates that societies that try to forcefully impose equal outcomes fail miserably. Regimes that repeatedly tried to enforce equal outcomes through aggressive redistribution in every case entrenched monstrously oppressive state control – "the price of history," as historian Tony Judt often bitingly put it. This suggests that the call for radical income redistribution to create "equal" outcomes is a deeply misguided prescription. Readers can refer to *The Commanding Heights* by Yergin and Stanislaw (2002) for an insightful account of why state-directed efforts to equalize outcomes create bad economic incentives, and in turn make large-scale cooperation unworkable.

What about the alternative version of the inequality argument – that inequality is driving institutional breakdown? At first blush, this argument appears convincing because the two major mechanisms it details are, separately, probably correct. Capitalism has historically been associated with increasing inequality, and rising inequality has tended to place de facto power in the hands of an elite who use it to demolish pluralist institutions. The flaw with this reasoning as far as the Western democracies are concerned is that levels of inequality have not been high enough to create the conditions for elite-driven institutional decay. Accordingly, Western populism is not an elite but a mass political movement. For example, prior to Trump's election, the US was largely perceived as a bastion of high-quality democratic institutions. In 2016, the US ranked in approximately the world's top 10 percent of the World Bank's World Governance Indicators for control of corruption, government effectiveness, regulatory quality, and rule of law.

The remaining economic arguments – trade shocks and the consequences of the GFC – are more useful. The key starting point from which to analyze these arguments is to note that they convincingly explain *some* portion of the populist wave. Trade shocks are decisively associated with the geography of populism within the US and the UK, and financial crises have repeatedly caused political extremism throughout history.

Rodrik sheds light on why trade shocks can theoretically be linked to populism. One might wonder, as he does, "why trade gets picked on so much by populists both on the right and the left. After all, imports are only one source of churn in labor markets, and typically not even the most important source" (2018: 18). The answer is that "it's one thing to lose your job to someone who competes under the same rules as you do. It's a different thing when you lose your job to someone who takes advantage of lax labor, environmental, tax, or safety standards in other countries … What arouses popular opposition … is perceived unfairness" (2018: 19). This conclusion provides a vital insight: it is not simply the job loss that matters, but the *fairness* of how and why a job is lost, and the support provided for recovery. People do not only care about the absolute magnitudes of final economic outcomes – they care deeply about whether those outcomes are fairly deserved.

It is thus plausible that populism could, at least in theory, result from job losses due to import competition. But we are presented with a puzzle, because the international geography of trade does not align well with populism. While the subnational geography of trade shocks in the US and the UK correspond to the incidence of populism, these countries are hardly the only ones that trade extensively with China. Murray (2017) considers the impact of Chinese import competition in the case of Canada. He finds that its impact was actually *more* severe than in the US. Whereas Acemoglu et al. (2016) conclude that 9.7 percent of US manufacturing job losses from 1999 to 2011 were attributable to Chinese import competition, the figure for Canada from 2001 to 2011 is a whopping 20.7 percent. In absolute terms, this translates to 560,000 job losses in the US versus approximately 105,000 in Canada – and thus a far larger share of the Canadian labor market, given that its population is roughly ten times smaller. Yet there is no Canadian Trump. Balsvik et al. (2015), in addition, find that roughly 10 percent of Norwegian manufacturing job losses from 1996 to 2007 can be explained by the China Shock. Figure 1.4 shows the growing importance of Chinese imports in a number of developed countries, some of which are conspicuously resistant to populism.

Murray provides a hint as to why this might be the case. Whereas Acemoglu et al. (2016) report no statistically significant evidence of US job recovery following the China Shock, Murray (2017) finds that there was at least 60 percent job recovery in Canada in the non-tradable sector. This finding suggests that it is not just the magnitude of the trade shock that matters, but, importantly, the way a country *responds* to the shock. Eriksson et al. (2019) provide supporting evidence for

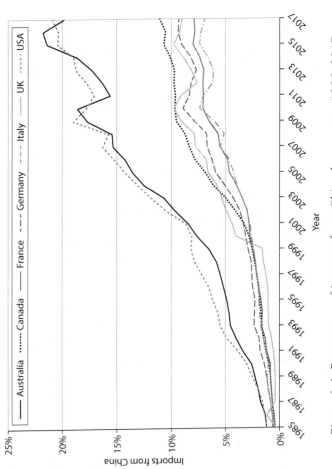

Figure 1.4: *Percentage of imports from China by country, 1985–2017*

this theory. They compare the China Shock in the US to earlier trade shocks spanning a century, and find dramatically different results depending on specific economic conditions. In particular, trade shocks are especially severe in places where the shocked industry is already in decline, wage levels are high, or levels of education are low. *The Economist* (2019a), which reviewed Eriksson et al.'s paper, commented that while "it may be tempting to conclude that America has paid too high a price for China's entry into the global trading system . . . A more helpful conclusion is that politicians should take more care to equip workers labouring far from the innovation frontier to adapt to shocks in their industries."

The academic literature on negative economic shocks to the labor market is very informative, but not because trade shocks are bogeymen spreading populism. A more compelling explanation, and a foundation for better policy, is that some societies are better at handling the fallout of economic shocks than others. In the US, the China Shock destroyed the precarious position of many American workers, and the state did little to guard against the blow or smooth the subsequent transition. That result created a deep sense of unfairness – Americans and their communities had been abandoned – which contributed in no small part to the wave of populism that has embroiled the US. Conversely, in Canada the initial shock was more severe, but the state supported workers far better and many were able to adjust and find new employment. Hence, Canada has not faced the same populist challenge.

Now let us consider the GFC and the policy response to it. Again, recall that these events almost certainly help explain part of contemporary populism. Losing one's home and enduring prolonged unemployment due to the self-interested actions of a narrow (and unpunished) financial elite is a sure recipe for political disruption. But the GFC only happened in 2008–9, whereas populism had already been growing for several decades. The GFC thus cannot by itself fully explain the rise of populism. The post-GFC political trends shown above in Figures 1.1–1.3 are, at face value, continuations, and accelerations of what was already happening. This is by no means proof of a connection, but it is suggestive and should prompt us to ask whether the nature of political discontent related to the GFC was qualitatively similar to that which was previously in the making.

What, then, colors the anger which resulted from the GFC? Funke et al. (2016) help answer this question, again by turning to history. They find that while financial crises result in political extremism, regular macroeconomic crises of the same magnitude *have no such effect at all*. The authors suggest that this may be because financial crises are viewed as the "inexcusable" result of a self-serving financial elite putting its own interests above those of broader society. This finding provides a critical insight into the nature of the political anger behind populism, and more profoundly into the human condition. People are not simply angry because the GFC left them worse off in absolute terms. They are angry because of the unfair way they were made and left poorer, and because of society's failure to punish those responsible. It was not a random occurrence, but a deliberate and preventable choice made by society's elites, in their own favor at the expense of everyone else.

Consider this in combination with the previous discussion about how different societies are prepared to respond to labor market shocks. These shocks occurred from approximately the 1990s onward, before the GFC. Anger was generated because of the particular *unfair* form of job losses, and the failure of society, and especially its elites, to choose policies that could have mitigated those losses. This outrage is strikingly similar in quality to that resulting from the GFC: in both cases political anger was induced not just because of how painful losses were in absolute terms, but critically because the losses were judged to be *unfair*.

This observation resonates with our definition of populism, as an anti-pluralist politics that stands against elites who have purportedly rigged the rules of society. Citizens may claim they want to rebalance those unfair rules because they have, in fact, had genuinely unfair economic experiences. Recall also the conclusion from the China Shock literature that a country's *vulnerability* to unfair job losses is the key link to populism, not so much the shock itself. The evidence suggests that unfair economic outcomes lead to populism, and that this happens through a country's propensity for economic fairness versus unfairness as dictated by its public policy.

While the six theories examined in this chapter are thus by themselves insufficient to explain populism, the synthesized conclusion from the most useful ones points toward a deeper hypothesis that constitutes the central argument of this book: populism results from public policy regimes that leave citizens vulnerable to economic unfairness. The problem of economic unfairness is wholly unrelated to prescriptions like deporting immigrants, regulating online speech, soaking the rich, or shutting down international trade. It is multifaceted, very difficult to treat, and will take at least a generation to repair.

2

The Fairness Instinct

Awards should be according to merit; for all men agree that what is just in distribution must be according to merit in some sense.

Aristotle, *Nicomachean Ethics*

Washington flourished, but the people did not share in its wealth . . . Politicians prospered, but the jobs left and factories closed . . . The forgotten men and women of our country will be forgotten no longer.

President Donald Trump, 2016

You could put half of Trump's supporters into what I call the basket of deplorables. Right? They're racist, sexist, homophobic, xenophobic, Islamophobic – you name it . . . they are irredeemable.

Hillary Clinton, 2016

Populist politicians across the developed world have risen to new electoral heights on the back of a powerful idea: fairness matters, and it is being violated. Political messaging like "Take Back Control" and "Drain the Swamp" resonate deeply among, to quote Trump, "forgotten people" who have been "left behind" in a "rigged system" run by out-of-touch elites. One American swing voter who ultimately supported Trump in the 2016 presidential election neatly articulated this truth to *The Boston Globe*:

> The government never helped me, but I was OK with that. I made mistakes, had some scary moments, and my wife worked at the local library to help out. I paid my bills, including my doctor bills. Now I see my tax dollars going to handouts for others who didn't work as hard as I did, and I can't afford my healthcare. Everyone is being taken care of but me. I feel left out, and it makes me feel that I want my country back. (Hessan 2016)

The political mainstream has in many ways struggled to respond to the populist complaint of unfairness. In several critical instances mainstream politicians have simply dismissed the legitimacy of concerns about an unfair economy and rising cultural dislocation. Instead, they vilified citizens holding populist points of view and were thus unable to speak to them in any meaningful way. Hillary Clinton's 2016 campaign famously hit an enormous pothole after she called supporters of Trump "deplorables," the same way Mitt Romney tripped up in the 2012 presidential election after calling 47 percent of Americans "entitled." Across the Atlantic, the Remain campaign leading up to the 2016 Brexit vote in the UK spoke of "financial apocalypse" (neatly reduced by the Leave campaign to "Project Fear") and positioned all the Leave messaging as purportedly stupid, thereby ignoring the anger that had been building up for many years. This refusal to seriously engage with the populist electorate was wrong-headed. As Eatwell and Goodwin (2018) demonstrate, populist voters have a host of very real grievances that, however crudely presented, speak to the problem of unfairness.

Yet even politicians who genuinely attempt to connect with the populist electorate have faced significant challenges. Corbyn's decisively left-wing electoral platform for the 2019 UK general election was in no small part designed to attract frustrated working-class voters. But this policy program, combined with his mishandling of the Brexit question, ultimately led those citizens to abandon the Labour Party in record-breaking droves. The 2020 Biden campaign carefully communicated moderate policy positions, but Republican messaging framed it instead in terms of the far-left ideas advocated by figures like Bernie Sanders and Alexandria Ocasio-Cortez. As a consequence the overwhelming victory that many imagined Democrats would enjoy dissipated. Biden only scraped together a knife-edge victory over Trump, with vote margins in the range of tens of thousands in critical swing states.

None of these campaigns fully addressed the core concerns of would-be populist voters because they did not understand the meaning or centrality of economic fairness. We will argue that the only way to reclaim populist sentiments for the liberal democratic mainstream, however, is to take populist voters *very* seriously and understand their concerns *very* precisely. Chapter 2 is thus devoted to exploring the nature of economic unfairness in detail. It will temporarily set aside the problem of populism and delve into what constitutes economic unfairness and how it came to be so important.

This chapter will first briefly review leading philosophical theories of economic justice. It will then present an alternative theory of economic fairness that citizens across the developed world largely subscribe to in practice. It will show that this standard has been promoted through biological and cultural evolution, and is now highly valued by citizens of contemporary liberal democracies. Finally, it will explore a key implication of the dynamic, evolutionary nature of fairness:

40

it is a moving target, and must be effectively managed as society evolves to avoid disaster. Armed with this understanding, subsequent chapters will be positioned to empirically connect economic unfairness to populism and analyze how policymakers can best rectify this problem.

Distributive Justice and Economic Fairness

A variety of contemporary philosophical theories, which fall under the umbrella of "distributive justice," try to explain how economic opportunities and outcomes should be best distributed. While the scope of this book permits only a very short overview of the main ideas in distributive justice, such a review is essential to understand the contemporary debate and assess the idea of economic fairness.

It is worth noting that economists often claim to be agnostic about distributive justice. Milton Friedman, one of the most influential modern economists, argued in a 1953 paper that economics should be purely "positive" and not "normative." That is, economists ought to work out the functional rules of the economy, much like a physicist might ascertain the laws of nature that govern electricity or thermodynamics. But he contended that economists should ignore moral questions of what *should* be done with the economy, and instead leave the matter to policymakers.

Despite the immense impact of Friedman's argument, in practice economics is largely framed by two schools of philosophical thought: utilitarianism and radical equality. The utilitarian view holds that society ought to be organized to maximize the net pleasure, happiness, and fulfillment of its citizens. In economics, utilitarianism assumes some "utility function" describing how a consumer's happiness – or, in the language of economists, "utility" – depends on certain material inputs, subject to certain constraints. The economist then solves a system of equations to determine how to maximize society's utility. A consequence of this approach is that economists often focus on growing a society's "economic pie" (often expressed as its Gross Domestic Product – GDP), in order to maximize aggregate welfare.

A key critique of utilitarianism is that mechanically maximizing society's net utility according to individual preferences could create dystopian outcomes. For example, under utilitarianism it could, in theory, be optimal for 90 percent of the population to enslave the other 10 percent. The net utility gained by the slaveowners would simply have to exceed that lost by the enslaved. Or a large ethnic majority could prefer for a small ethnic minority to live in dire poverty, making it "optimal" to enforce that outcome. Eventualities like these have, of course, played out repeatedly in history, but few today would consider them to be desirable – let alone optimal.

Some relatively heterodox – but now increasingly widely accepted – economic views of distributive justice are instead grounded in radical equality, which advocates strictly equal material outcomes. It is now routine to read about the danger of sky-high inequality from leading economists, and politicians peddle policy prescriptions to equalize outcomes often for the sake of income and wealth equality alone. Calls to outlaw billionaires through aggressive wealth taxes are a classic example that have recently featured in the political life of many high-income countries.

The problems with radical equality are well known. The driving inspiration of twentieth-century communist regimes was to create equal economic outcomes. Their efforts to eliminate private property and collectivize agriculture were enforced by the state through increasingly illiberal and criminal means that ultimately sacrificed life and personal freedom, not to mention economic efficiency. The twentieth century proved over and over again that the road to enforced equal outcomes is lined with both millions of corpses and badly built cars. One thus has to care a great deal more about relative than about absolute welfare to accept equal economic outcomes.

Outside economics, political philosophers have contributed rich theories to the debate on distributive justice. It is some wonder, in a sense, that economics has largely failed to take these perspectives into account. One such family of theories is desert-based distributive justice, where "desert" refers to an individual's deservingness. According to this perspective, people are naturally entitled to the fruits of their labor. Modern desert-based theories of distributive justice argue that rewarding people according to a standard of deservingness maximizes the "social product," or society's standard of living, by incentivizing productive contributions. Importantly, desert-based theories do not claim to fully explain economic justice. They hold that desert-based reward applies for "capable" members of society, and that additional principles are needed to deal with those who cannot contribute much (for example children, the very elderly, and the severely incapacitated).

The most important critique of desert-based distributive justice is that people do not choose key inputs to their own productivity, particularly genetic advantages and family. This counterargument, pervasive in philosophical discourse today, holds that people should only be rewarded for what they personally choose.

The previous theories notwithstanding, the contemporary philosophical debate about distributive justice is largely centered around John Rawls's *A Theory of Justice* (2009), and the important replies that book elicited. Rawls contends that justice should be understood as fairness, and argues for particular rules necessary for a fair society. He argues that if people are made to design rules for society in the abstract without actually knowing their potential characteristics in terms of race, gender, intelligence, and more – a position he calls being behind the "veil of ignorance" – they will choose basic civil liberties in addition to two particular rules of distributive justice. First, anyone with the same talents and abilities, and the same willingness to use them, should have the same chance of success. This requires substantive equal opportunity, which entails both freedom from discrimination and access to the public goods needed to give everyone a real chance at success. Second, insofar as social and economic inequalities exist, they ought to be of the greatest benefit to the least advantaged members of society – an idea known as the Difference Principle. Thus, if the economy creates unequal outcomes but also creates an economic surplus that is used to lift the living standards of the poorest members of society, then, according to Rawls, that social structure is just. In contrast, the rich should not get richer in a way that is neutral or deleterious to the poor.

The previously mentioned theories often disagree with Rawls. A desert-based conception would hold that someone could deserve to get richer even if it does not benefit others. Utilitarians, similarly, would argue that making one person richer with no consequences for others increases society's overall utility. Radical egalitarians would hold that Rawls does not go nearly far enough because he does not call for substantially equalized economic outcomes.

Another school of thought, luck egalitarianism, elaborates on Rawls's arguments for equal opportunity. Luck egalitarians hold that people should only be rewarded for their "ambitions," or their choices and actions, and never for their "endowments," or things they cannot control, such as genetics, family wealth, or whether they get sick. The "unlucky," in this sense, should be no worse off than the "lucky." In this view people who become poor due to their own choices should not be compensated, while people who are unlucky in nonmaterial ways (such as becoming severely disabled) may require substantial material compensation. This is an important departure from Rawls's Difference Principle, which in and of itself does not guarantee this kind of redress.

Finally, communitarians take issue with Rawls's construction of universal principles from behind the veil of ignorance. They retort that no society can abstract from itself, and that justice is strongly informed by communal culture and history. Not only does the veil of ignorance not exist, but when humans agree on rules of justice the rationale stems in important ways from communities and not simply from individual desires. Thus, from the communitarian perspective, Rawls's approach may be inherently irrelevant and incoherent.

As such, there are diverse contemporary philosophical perspectives on distributive justice, which, out of necessity, the preceding discussion has only touched the surface of. As we will see, however, some are considerably more relevant to the economic unfairness that drives populism than are others.

An Evolutionary Theory of Economic Fairness

A philosopher asks "What is fair?" and argues for some particular (often supposedly ideal) standard of fairness regardless of whether most people would actually endorse it. Not so for a democratic policymaker, who is accountable to all their citizens. While abstract philosophical ideas can inform the way a policymaker understands human nature, they ultimately ask "Do citizens on the whole agree that society is fair?" The same logic governs any appropriate policy response to the populist complaint of unfairness. Policymakers cannot simply theorize how fairness should function in an ideal society; they must seek to understand how citizens across the developed world construct economic fairness *in practice*.

Some would contend that this is an impossible task because human morality varies so widely. As communitarians point out, different societies have wildly conflicting standards of justice. For example, Islam, Confucianism, and Western liberalism have largely different and incompatible visions for the role of women in the economy and society. By the same token, individuals also have extraordinarily different standards of economic justice. Within the same society one can find enthusiasts of hard-left and hard-right economic systems with little to no common ground.

We certainly will not make the case for an ideal formulation of economic fairness, nor a universal one that every individual across time and space would endorse. Our focus is considerably narrower: we will argue for one particular set of moral rules pertaining to economic fairness that is widely subscribed to in the developed world today. This standard of economic fairness may not fully account for economic justice in an ideal or historical society. Nevertheless, it aims to explain a vital moral sentiment that has come to be shared by the bulk of citizens in modern market democracies.

The starting point to deduce this standard of economic fairness, and explain why it is so widespread in modern high-income societies, lies in the evolutionary forces that shape humanity. In particular, evolution continuously optimizes human behavior according to our species' (and especially its most prosperous societies') key competitive advantage: complex cooperation. Without sophisticated, large-scale cooperation our species would be another animal fated to live or die as the environment dictates, rather than able to shape its own fate. Harari (2014: 28) explains that humans "can cooperate in extremely flexible ways with countless numbers of strangers. That's why Sapiens rule the world, whereas ants eat our leftovers and chimps are locked up in zoos and research laboratories."

It is very important to understand that evolution, as discussed here, is not purely a biological phenomenon relegated to humanity's long prehistory. Human behavior is also deeply influenced by ongoing cultural evolution that results from new ideas and modes of social organization. Charles Darwin highlighted the significance of cultural evolution in *The Descent of Man* (2004 [1871]: 154) when he wrote that "if some man in a tribe, more sagacious than the others, invented a new snare or weapon, or other means of attack or defence, the plainest self-interest, without the assistance of much reasoning power, would prompt the other members to imitate him; and all would thus profit."

The rules of human behavior that shape cooperation are directly governed by the forces of evolution. This, in and of itself, is an astounding fact. The common name for the rules humans use to cooperate is "morality," and these rules are often perceived to derive from some exogenous, absolute truth that falls like manna from heaven. In fact, the moral rules people endorse or reject are a direct result of biological and cultural evolution, and they have evolved specifically to optimize cooperation. This conclusion is well-established in the relevant academic literature. Among many possible examples, Tomasello and Vaish (2013) argue that "human morality arose evolutionarily as a set of skills and motives for cooperating with others," and Curry (2016: 29) explicitly identifies that "morality turns out to be a collection of biological and cultural solutions to the problems of cooperation and conflict."

Human cooperation is, of course, an extremely complex and dynamic problem, and morality is accordingly multifaceted. Haidt (2012) identifies care/harm, loyalty/betrayal, authority/subversion, sanctity/degradation, liberty/oppression, and fairness/cheating as a few key dimensions of human morality. The specific formulations of these values can vary immensely across different societies past and present, depending on how they cooperate.

Nevertheless, evolution consistently selects moral rules of economic cooperation according to a few important principles. In the broadest sense, economic cooperation can be understood as a strategic game. The participants all seek material gain, which helps to ensure that they survive, thrive, and pass on their genes. Collaborating with others can produce many more resources than working in isolation, so group cooperation enhances fitness and survival. But resources are finite, so cooperation also has a deadly serious competitive edge. If a participant does not like the current rules, they may seek to change them, through force if necessary. Too much disruption, and all members have a lesser chance of passing on their biological and cultural genes. Thus the best rules of economic cooperation, which are promoted through evolution, are those which create *prosperous* and *strategically stable* outcomes. Under these conditions, cooperation is sufficiently beneficial so that group members have little reason to take on the risks associated with overturning the current system of rules.

On the whole, cooperation has been a vital part of the human experience spanning hunter-gatherer, agricultural, industrial, and postindustrial societies. We should thus expect to find basic recognition of the most critical moral rules of cooperation among people from many different walks of life. Nevertheless, human societies both historical and contemporary differ quite dramatically by the degree to which they engage in genuine, large-scale economic cooperation. For instance, early-stage societies might cooperate closely within a select group but apply alternative strategies such as exclusion and domination toward outsiders – treating them no differently than they would wild or domesticated animals. There are many historical examples where one group of humans opted to attack rather than cooperate with another group, or somehow subjugate them in an immutable vertical hierarchy.

The most prosperous societies today, in contrast, practice intense complex cooperation. Modern, rich, globalized countries are primarily the result of millions and millions of people working together rather than practicing exclusion or domination. This is no coincidence; as Acemoglu and Robinson (2012) overwhelmingly demonstrate, inclusive institutions that support mass cooperation rather than domination are perhaps the single most important enabler of long-term societal prosperity. Crucially, this means that as societies progress to cooperate more intensively on larger scales, we should expect them to promote moral rules that facilitate cooperation above conflicting alternatives. It is no use hanging on to xenophobia or strict deference to elites when your key survival strategy is instead to cooperate with people from all race and class backgrounds. That is an important reason why modern high-income countries reliably hold particular moral sentiments: they have all evolved to rely on ultra-intensive, large-scale cooperation, which critically depends on certain moral rules.

We propose that a specific rule, often called "fairness," especially enables complex economic cooperation and is widely endorsed in the developed world today. Intuitively, fairness stipulates that the rewards from cooperation should be principally divided according to individual contribution. This rule is similar but (as will be seen) not fully interchangeable with philosophical theories of desert-based distributive justice. Importantly, when someone violates the fairness rule for their own benefit, they are considered a "cheater," often with commensurately severe consequences.

In more precise terms, economic cooperation is a complex game for which "fairness" is part of a relatively stable and prosperous game-theoretical solution. Participants chiefly allocate the rewards from cooperation according to each person's marginal productivity, but – crucially – they only do so if a person's actions are compatible with long-term cooperation. It will generally not be considered fair if an agent expropriates rewards or opportunities from others, because other agents will, in the long term, be incentivized to discontinue cooperation or alter its rules (perhaps violently).

There are many mathematical explanations for why exactly fairness makes cooperation optimally stable and prosperous. Debove (2015) reviews thirty-six such theories, which variously suggest biological, cultural, or mixed mechanisms for the development of fairness. He additionally provides original evidence showing that "when individuals can choose their cooperative partners, meritocratic distributions emerge as the best strategy."

This book does not itself formulate fairness in mathematically precise terms. It instead proceeds in the vein of scholars like Guriev (2018) and Rodrik (2018), who provide intuition about economic fairness that is sufficiently generalizable to be relevant to policymakers. As Sen (2009) argues, a technically and philosophically perfect definition of fairness is unnecessary for and even counterproductive to practically advancing fairness in society. For intuition as to why fairness is so advantageous one might consider the following passage from Starmans et al. (2017):

> When individuals can choose the people with whom they interact for mutually beneficial tasks, cooperative individuals gain benefits from being included and selfish individuals lose out on those benefits by being shunned. But individuals who are too cooperative – too generous – run the risk of being taken advantage of by others. So a balance must be struck. To treat everyone equally would entail penalization of more productive individuals when they collaborate with less productive individuals relative to highly productive individuals. In contrast with equality, fairness allows individuals with different levels of productivity to share the benefits of their collaboration proportionately. This focus on fairness is particularly important for humans (compared with even our closest evolutionary relatives), due to the critical importance of collaboration in human hunting and foraging.

This understanding of fairness means it can be violated in a few notable ways. First, an individual is often considered to be a cheater not only if they *directly* expropriate others, but also if they do so *indirectly*. For example, a financier who profits from speculation but in doing so crashes the economy will be judged a cheater by others, in much the same way as a thief will be, as Foroohar (2016) argues. That is why, as explained in Chapter 1, financial crises have been persistently associated with popular discontent throughout history. This distinction is important because it disagrees with certain neoliberal desert-based conceptions of distributive justice, which argue that people should be rewarded according to *any* near-term economic value they create – regardless of its future consequences. In reality, evolution pushes strategic agents to despise both direct and indirect adverse consequences. Attempting to ignore indirect consequences is strategically unstable.

Second, fairness can be violated when rewards and opportunities are allocated according to a standard that is not intrinsically related to a person's ability to create value. If, in a group of cooperating individuals, one person gets higher rewards and better opportunities, due, for example, to their hair color, other agents have good reason to rebel against such an arbitrary rule. Doing so will more closely connect reward to contribution, creating incentives that lead to better outcomes for many group members.

A crucial conclusion follows: fairness entails equal opportunity. It is not fair that someone from a privileged background should automatically get higher rewards, because that privilege does not intrinsically drive productivity. The educational opportunities given to the elite might, for instance, be extended to others, who could then become just as (if not more) productive.

At the same time, however, fairness requires that individuals are rewarded for intrinsic talents that assist productivity, even if those talents are uncontrollable.

Some luck egalitarians would disagree, pointing out that nobody can choose their genetically determined intelligence or strength. The forces of evolution, however, don't operate by such a principle. Non-innate drivers of productivity, like education, can be redistributed. Strategic agents thus have strong incentives to see that their children get these kinds of opportunities, by some form of redistribution if necessary. But barring nightmarish science-fiction scenarios, nobody can redistribute genetics or accidental genius.

This leads to the third point. The only way to wholly avoid rewarding innate, uncontrollable talent is to equalize outcomes; all the evidence, however, is that aggressively equalizing outcomes breaks the relationship between reward and contribution, with potentially catastrophic consequences. Evolution thus squarely rejects enforced equal outcomes, and treats them as atrociously unfair.

Economic fairness as described here sits in an interesting place among standard philosophical theories of distributive justice. Of particular note, it sharply disagrees with key aspects of the two that largely frame modern economics. The enforced equal outcomes required by radical equality are totally incompatible with fairness. Utilitarianism, too, cannot readily substitute for fairness because it focuses on aggregate outcomes and does not sufficiently emphasize the game-theoretical nature of strategic interaction between cooperating agents. Maximizing aggregate outcomes in a way that systematically penalizes certain members of society creates deep incentives for those underdogs to throw off their masters. The neoliberal, short-termist, "market is always right" formulation of utilitarianism is especially incompatible with fairness because it strongly discounts these kinds of dynamics.

Luck egalitarianism poses an especially striking contrast with economic fairness that is worth exploring further. While this school of thought claims that people should be rewarded for their controllable "ambitions" but never for their uncontrollable "endowments," this division is crude and inaccurate from the perspective of economic fairness. Instead of asking whether a factor is controllable or uncontrollable, economic fairness first asks whether it genuinely influences productivity. For example, a person's skin or hair color does not affect their economic productivity in any way, so it is obviously unfair to allocate economic rewards on that basis.

Second, economic fairness examines whether a factor confers *transferable* or *nontransferable* advantages. On the one hand, family wealth is a major example of a characteristic that confers *transferable* advantages. While it delivers superior access to education, healthcare, and other goods that improve productivity, this wealth can also be taxed so that others too enjoy these advantages. If access to these transferable factors is redistributed across society, then every strategic agent can feel confident that they and their children will have the opportunity to reach their productive potential.

In stark contrast, factors that confer *nontransferable* advantages are fair determinants of economic rewards. Evolutionary agents cannot, of course, demand that other members of their community hand over their genetically determined intelligence. It is not just futile, nonsensical, and dangerous to attack nontransferable determinants of productivity; in fact, most societies *celebrate* those factors because it is better to work with smarter and stronger cooperative partners.

Communitarianism, on the other hand, serves as a compelling foil for the evolutionary nature of fairness. In one sense, communitarians have a point in that group dynamics critically shape morality. Economic fairness is not the pure result of individual decisions or introspection, but rather the way that individual incentives strategically interact with one another. At the same time, it is important to recognize that the very same dynamics have made certain values extremely widespread in modern market democracies. It is useful to acknowledge the general applicability of those values, even if there are other societies they might not fully apply to.

Desert-based and Rawlsian distributive justice, notably, have important areas of overlap with economic fairness. Fairness chiefly allocates rewards according to contribution, a form of "desert," albeit only insofar as doing so is game-theoretically stable. It also stands by Rawls's appeal to equal opportunity – that anybody with the same talents and abilities, and the same willingness to use them, should have the same chances of success. At the same time, it is not clear that the Difference Principle follows from economic fairness. It is not obviously always strategically unstable for some group members to receive higher rewards if poorer members are unaffected.

Of course, fairness is hardly the only behavior or value that evolution promotes, and by itself the fairness rule is not a complete account of economic justice in the developed world today. An example of another important value is solidarity. There is a compelling moral perspective that all humans have some baseline level of deservingness as sentient beings. According to this value, even those who are incapable of contributing much to society materially should be taken care of. It is not difficult to imagine how solidarity may help optimize cooperation to enhance survival and reproduction. For instance, if villagers agree to take care of each other's children in the event they are orphaned, each parent can be assured a greater chance that their genes will be passed on regardless of the bad luck they might encounter. Solidarity also helps smooth over shocks; if someone is temporarily ill and unproductive, it is worth helping them recover so they can be productive again. Finally, solidarity may enhance social cohesion. People may be likelier to cooperate if they know other group members will always look out for them.

All of this is well and good, and solidarity is likely important for effective cooperation. But that does not undermine the overarching importance of fairness. To a significant extent, solidarity is wholly compatible with fairness: imposing a floor on living standards does not inhibit the "fair" distribution of rewards according to contribution above that floor. It is thus possible to retain the most important incentives that fairness engenders.

Evolutionary Evidence for Fairness

Having outlined the logic that explains why economic fairness is widely valued in the developed world today, let us turn to the empirical proof that this is true. At each major stage of humanity's history there is evidence that evolutionary forces promote fairness. The differential success and failure of societies that respectively embrace rather than eschew fairness creates a powerful selection mechanism, and has culminated in widespread adherence to fairness in modern market democracies.

While we cannot directly study the cognition of our distant ancestors, we can glean information about early biological selection for fairness in other ways. For instance, there is evidence for a fairness instinct in our biological relatives. In a highly entertaining experiment, which you can find on YouTube, Brosnan and De Waal

(2003) train capuchin monkeys to trade stone tokens with humans for treats. To begin the experiment, a monkey is first given a slice of cucumber in exchange for a token. So far so good – the monkey is happy to eat the cucumber. But next it is shown another monkey which, upon exchanging a token, receives a grape rather than a cucumber slice (which both the monkeys in question and these authors regard as a far tastier reward).

The original monkey is perplexed. Have the payoffs in the game changed? It repeats the task of exchanging a token with the human experimenter. But lo and behold, it is given yet another cucumber slice. For a moment it pauses and examines its reward. Then it throws the cucumber slice at the human and shakes the wall of its cage in what can only be described as visceral, furry rage.

One might draw the simple conclusion that the monkeys are opposed to unequal outcomes. But critically, when the monkeys are, alternatively, shown their compatriots receiving grapes *without* having to exchange a token, the rate of noncompliance (cucumber-throwing) is *even higher*. This outcome would have been impossible if the monkeys were uniformly opposed to all unequal outcomes, in which case conceptions of different levels of deservingness would not enter into the equation. The capuchin monkeys are evidently instead very sensitive to the relationship between relative rewards and relative effort – they are driven by fairness, and detest being "cheated."

Importantly, a similar fairness instinct has also been observed in human children and even infants. For example, Sloane et al. (2012) show that 1–2-year-old babies expect more resources to be allocated to those who have done more work. Kenward and Dahl (2011) demonstrate that 3-year-old children prefer to allocate greater rewards to helpful rather than aggressive puppets. Starmans et al. (2017) note that 6-year-olds prefer to allocate additional resources to someone who has done more work, even when they have the option to distribute rewards equally. At such early stages of development, nature arguably outweighs nurture in important respects, giving a cleaner perspective on biologically rather than culturally programmed behavior. The fact that the fairness instinct is found both in the behavior of young humans and in our biological relatives demonstrates that it is hard-wired into our DNA.

A key consequence of the fairness instinct is that humans are broadly sensitive to economic fairness. Starmans et al. (2017) review the behavioral science literature on relative rewards, and conclude that "there is no evidence that people are bothered by economic inequality itself. Rather, they are bothered by something that is often confounded with inequality: economic unfairness." The authors explain that people consistently expect and prefer for higher rewards to go to those who have exerted more effort or used greater skill to do a job more effectively. After taking this preference into account, *people do not systematically care about how unequal outcomes are; they care about whether outcomes are fair.* This position is hardly an outlier in the literature. Debove (2015) notes that "it is well accepted in the behavioral sciences that people prefer income distributions with strong work–salary correlations, prefer to give more to individuals whose input is more valuable, and favor meritocratic distributions as a whole in both micro- and macro-justice contexts."

To explain this pattern of behavior, Starmans et al. (2017) highlight two well-known research findings. First, they consider the "ultimatum" game. The results from this game are often interpreted to support the contention that people dislike unequal outcomes. In fact, that conclusion is short-sighted and false. The ultimatum game is really about fairness.

In the ultimatum game, two people must divide a reward, for example $100, between them. Person A gets to choose how much money each participant gets, and person B either accepts the distribution or rejects it, in which case nobody gets anything. In practice, when person A chooses an increasingly unequal distribution of rewards, person B is increasingly likely to reject the distribution. The common (but false) conclusion from this finding is that people must dislike unequal outcomes. Yet studies such as the one by Norton and Ariely (2011) in fact find that when people are asked what society's income and wealth inequality should look like, they nearly always prefer a substantial degree of inequality.

How can this be?

The answer is that people do not prefer unconditionally equal outcomes, but prize *fair* economic outcomes – unequal or otherwise. In the ultimatum game, the reward distribution is almost arbitrary. Person A has been given the power to choose, but nobody has done anything to deserve a higher reward than anyone else. Thus, in this *particular* case unequal outcomes happen to be unfair, because each player is equally deserving. But the real principle behind the game is not a systematic preference for equal outcomes – it is a systematic preference for *fair* outcomes. Accordingly, people overwhelmingly feel that society should have *unequal* economic outcomes because they know that individual talent and effort vary immensely, and it is fair to reward people according to their contributions.

However, as discussed, fairness is hardly the only instinct that promotes survival, especially in early-stage human societies. Humans are also biologically programmed to greedily hoard resources, exclude outsiders, and seek a strictly dominant alpha status, for example, all of which directly conflicts with fairness. Biology alone thus implies an important role for fairness, but does not necessarily suggest that it is systematically revered and aspired to.

Cultural evolution in relatively early-stage societies, however, further reinforces the importance of fairness. Acemoglu and Robinson (2020) eloquently demonstrate how small-scale societies that do not reward value creation fail to get off the ground. They highlight the Tiv tribe of Nigeria as an example: "Preventing powerful individuals from becoming too dominant ... was a major concern for Tiv society ... [Tiv norms] made them suspicious of power and willing to take action against those building their power" (2020: 54). The Tiv were, in fact, so suspicious of power that they accused people who had accumulated social or material advantages of outright witchcraft. It is not difficult to imagine how this might hold back societal progress:

> The caged economy of the Tiv had obvious adverse consequences. Markets are critical for an efficient organization of the economy and for prosperity. But they weren't permitted to function among the Tiv ... The institutions of Tiv society created little incentive for capital accumulation ... even saving could lead one to be accused of [accumulating too much power], so the fear of retribution made accumulation too dangerous. (2020: 104)

The consequence of adopting a value system that refused to reward value creation was that Tiv society could not develop, and has remained stuck in extreme poverty. This prevented the evolutionary spread of Tiv cultural traits, namely their unfair delinking of economic rewards from value creation.

There is also quantitative evidence on cultural selection for fairness in our early history. Henrich et al. (2010) collect data on fifteen very different populations across the globe, which variously survive by foraging, fishing, hunting, horticulture, pastoralism, farming, and wage work. They run the ultimatum game in each of these societies and find that "market integration (measured as the percentage of purchased calories) positively covaries with fairness." That is, individuals in societies which prefer to allocate economic rewards according to fairness obtain a higher share of food by purchasing it from others.

Markets are an incredible tool for prosperity. If the cultural trait of fairness is a critical input to the adoption of markets, it means fairness must be highly predisposed to spread and reproduce. In the words of Henrich et al., "larger and more-complex societies prospered and *spread* to the degree that their norms and institutions effectively sustained successful interaction in ever-widening socioeconomic spheres" (2010: 1480; emphasis added).

Cultural selection for fairness is not just limited to the early stages of societal development. There is powerful evidence of evolutionary selection within the past few hundred years. Consider, on the one hand, the relative failure of large-scale societies that do not substantially reward people based on the economic value they create. Communism, a system which attempted to reward people equally (but in practice actually rewarded people according to their loyalty and political status), is an obvious example. The economic and political problems of communism resulted in generations of economic stagnation and hardship. This reward system was egregiously unfair and, importantly, has largely disappeared from the world. That is, the communist cultural gene faced an evolutionary dead end and has become almost extinct.

Conversely, consider the incredible success and persistence of societies that amply reward contribution. Countries that embrace the free market, which in many important ways rewards value creation, have prospered. Beginning in approximately the eighteenth century, the capitalist European powers experienced phenomenal economic growth. In a seminal paper Acemoglu et al. (2005) demonstrate that a mix of pre-existing institutional constraints on monarchies and trans-Atlantic trade led to the rise of a powerful merchant class in some European countries, which in turn moved to entrench protections for the free market. This institutional development explains to a substantial extent why certain European countries became so rich. In the words of the authors: "Rapid economic development [in Europe] did not begin until the emergence of political institutions providing secure property rights to a broader segment of society and allowing free entry into profitable businesses" (2005: 550). Average incomes were lifted to levels many times higher than those found elsewhere, and this same pattern tended to be repeated by these countries' settler colonies, such as the US, Canada, Australia, and New Zealand. From the twentieth century onwards, the Asian Tiger economies likewise found prosperity through rewarding value creation in the market, although notably often with significant use of complementary industrial policy (World Bank 1993). Japan, Taiwan, Hong Kong, South Korea, and Singapore – whose decisive market reforms were central to their economic growth – are now the wealthiest countries in the region, and there is some evidence of take-off among a number of Southeast Asian economies that have embraced more efficient markets.

The contrast between cultural genes which go extinct after eschewing reward according to contribution and those that thrive after embracing it creates an important third effect: the *spread* of fairness through force and imitation. There are a number of examples of this evolutionary process in recent history. For instance, the post-Soviet world, which was previously mired in unfair enforced equal outcomes, has largely converted to the greater fairness of the market mechanism. Figure 2.1 shows that virtually every post-Soviet and post-Eastern bloc country has experienced higher GDP per capita growth (in numerous cases dramatically so) after transitioning away from communism. Of course, many of these countries remain notoriously corrupt and inefficient by developed-world standards; the point is not that they have all yet reached the highest echelons of effective cooperation, but that they have been put on a decidedly better path by moving away from communism and toward the market.

China likewise in significant (albeit limited) ways turned away from communism and toward rewarding value creation. Its post-1979 market reforms, illustrated in Deng Xiaoping's pragmatic maxim that "it doesn't matter whether the cat is black or white as long as it catches mice," critically contributed to its take-off growth, which is why it is now one of the world's largest economies. The rise of other East and Southeast Asian economies, such as those mentioned, can also be understood through evolutionary mimicry. First, Japan imitated the market competition of the Western world through the Meiji reforms; then the Asian Tiger economies imitated Japan; and now Southeast Asian countries such as Malaysia and Thailand are imitating the Asian Tigers.

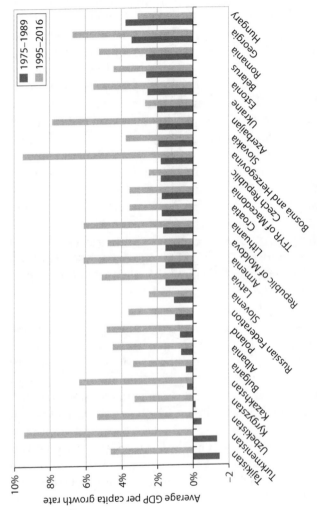

Figure 2.1: Average real GDP per capita growth rates, pre- and post-transition

Source: Bolt et al. 2018

The Fairness Instinct

To intuitively understand how fairness gets promoted through cultural evolution, one might contrast it with conflicting values. Consider loyalty to dominant elites. The abuse of power by elites to extract resources from the population is a common feature of many developing societies. It is manifested in phenomena such as corruption, rent-seeking, and outright expropriation. While this practice directly conflicts with fairness – value is extracted instead of created – it is often politically sustainable when large de facto power imbalances exist in society, for instance between peasants and an emperor.

Fundamentally, it is worth trying to change the rules of society if you have a high chance of success and the resultant change delivers a high payoff. The existence of a power imbalance means the weak have a low chance of successfully changing the rules, and there is thus an opportunity for the strong to extract value from the weak. Yet, the strong cannot be too exploitative or the weak will take that low chance. A bad equilibrium emerges in which a significant degree of unfairness is possible insofar as the weak do not have sufficient incentive to risk the fallout of rebellion.

In this situation, loyalty to elites can easily be normalized and entrenched in culture at the direct expense of fairness. Unquestioning loyalty to the monarch was a common feature of very many historical societies, and is still expressed in a number of countries today. The Chinese Communist Party, for example, deliberately cultivates a nationalist culture which asserts devotion to the party and its leadership. It may in fact be rational for individuals stuck in these despotic societies to prioritize loyalty to elites above fairness; disloyalty is likely to incur the wrath of the powerful, while loyalty may curry their favor.

But when these kinds of power relationships exist, only a moderate degree of societal prosperity can ever be achieved. The reasons are spelled out in detail by Acemoglu and Robinson (2012, 2020), and are strongly supported by their empirical research. A summary of the argument is presented in *The Narrow Corridor* (2020: 125):

> Despotic though it may be, the [authoritarian] state can prevent fighting, resolve conflicts, impose laws that help economic transactions, invest in public infrastructure, and help generate economic activity ... But it is inherently fragile and limited ... it does not activate and nurture the most productive aspects of society – its ability to freely function, generate broad-based opportunities and incentives for economic activity, and bring forth investment, experimentation, and innovation.

That is why a high-income authoritarian country has never existed. Middle-income status is achievable in these kinds of societies, for instance as seen in the USSR during the Cold War, or in China today – which, it bears remembering, has an official GDP per capita of just approximately $10,000, comparable to Mexico and Kazakhstan. (Of course, China's official GDP statistics are widely considered to be inflated for propaganda purposes; Premier Li Keqiang famously said in 2007 that they are "man-made.") But a slowdown inevitably results. Fully fledged prosperity has never been attained under authoritarian rule (barring the small number of petrostates with high levels of per capita income that nevertheless cannot be understood as robust models of human development) and probably never will be.

There is, of course, much analysis about how China has *already* entered an economic slowdown thanks to its authoritarianism. To give one example, an opinion piece by Broadman (2019) in *The Financial Times* commented that "the growth rate of the Chinese economy has been on a steady decline over the past 10 years" and that "the squeeze is largely self-induced. It stems from the lack of further reform . . . In an economy still heavily dominated by the state." A concrete and prominent example of this problem was in the news in late 2020 when Chinese President Xi Jinping halted Jack Ma's Ant Group's record-breaking $37 billion initial public offering. Apparently, Ma insulted government regulators and President Xi with comments about an overbearing government and the insistence that success was not just a product of the state. Many commentators added that Xi has been increasingly anxious about the ascendance of successful private businesses because they pose a direct challenge to the authority of the Communist Party and his rule.

As such, the world's most prosperous societies that engage in the highest levels of complex cooperation cannot and do not prioritize unquestioning loyalty to despotic elites. They instead have come to favor fairness. Allocating rewards according to value creation unlocks the highest echelons of economic growth. Systematically allocating rewards to elites does not.

Next consider xenophobia. Judgment based on group identity historically enhanced survival for small communities because there were out-groups with which they did not cooperate, and instead competed against. That is an important reason why group judgment has been such a common feature of human societies, and why substantial discrimination persists in very many countries today. In some societies, discrimination based on group identity has in fact been a key feature of culture for many centuries, as seen, for instance, in India's caste system.

But of course, xenophobia inhibits the most complex forms of cooperation. A person's potential productivity has absolutely nothing to do with their group identity, so society is most productive when identity does not hold back an individual's opportunity to create value. Accordingly, the world's most developed societies emphasize tolerance of different group identities – for example, they tend to be highly racially tolerant compared to other countries according to the 2012 World Values Survey. Evolutionary optimization for complex cooperation has rightly winnowed out a great degree of racism in the developed world, along with judgment based on other factors unrelated to productivity such as gender and sexuality. Fairness is emphasized instead, where a person is economically evaluated in terms of their potential to create value.

The consequence of this long process of evolutionary selection is that fairness is widely valued throughout the developed world today. Biological evolution has stamped the fairness instinct on every human as a foundational enabler of complex cooperation, and cultural evolution has reinforced fairness through the success of societies, small and large, which practice it. The most successful and prosperous societies today overwhelmingly depend on complex cooperation, for which fairness is an absolutely essential ingredient.

The Eternal Threat of Unfairness

It is very important to note, however, that evolution is hardly static and neither is the way that fairness operates. As societies face internal and external change, they must often reckon with the way they apply fairness and relate it to other values and behaviors. The everlasting challenge is that technological, environmental, economic, political, social, and cultural change make fairness a moving target. There are many bumps in the road which can create new winners, who may then attempt to unfairly entrench their powers. By the same token, different people in the same society can have diametrically opposed ideas concerning the valuation and interpretation of fairness – especially when new societal dynamics come into play. For example, many societies now tax greenhouse gas emission because they recognize its unfair consequences for others. But this was not true during the Industrial Revolution. Scientific progress and the recognition of the threat of climate change has forced a novel, extremely serious evaluation of whether certain polluting forms of economic production are fair.

While evolutionary forces push toward fairness, its advancement is hardly inexorable. There is always the threat of derailment from new shocks and would-be "cheaters." Society must thus be ever-vigilant, doggedly pursuing fairness – even and especially if that means considering the merits of a perspective we might instinctively dismiss. If it does not, then some citizens may come to consider others to be "cheaters" who violate fairness for their own benefit. The resultant societal friction mounts gradually, then suddenly, as the slow build-up to the post-2015 explosion of populism demonstrates.

Armed with this understanding of economic fairness, we can draw two key conclusions. First, the populist charge that society is unfair ought to be taken very, very seriously. Fairness is a central concern for citizens across the developed world that, if badly managed, can explode into catastrophic violence. Second, we should understand this complaint very precisely: populist anger is plausibly directed at perceived "cheaters" who unfairly set the rules of society for their own benefit, in a way that prevents other people from succeeding through legitimate value creation. Given that a core feature of populism is its anger at elites who have purportedly rigged the system, this would not be surprising. As will be seen in the next chapter, economic unfairness is, in fact, statistically connected to global populism – far more so than the scapegoats that dominate popular and academic discourse.

3

Economic Unfairness and the Rise of Populism

> Inequality is not the same thing as unfairness; and, to my mind, it is the latter that has incited so much political turmoil in the rich world today. Some of the processes that generate inequality are widely seen as fair. But others are deeply and obviously unfair, and have become a legitimate source of anger and disaffection.
>
> Angus Deaton, Nobel Laureate in Economics

So far this book has presented the theoretical foundations of economic unfairness and some circumstantial evidence that it fuels populism. As argued, there is powerful proof that most citizens of modern market democracies care deeply about fairness. Populist language also squarely targets perceived unfairness, where plutocratic elites allegedly tilt society's playing field against everyone else. What's more, mishandled economic shocks that convincingly contributed to populism in certain settings, like the GFC and the China Shock, arguably have led to political upheaval by specifically creating unfair economic outcomes. In and of themselves, these links are compelling and suggestive.

The political economy literature on economic fairness, nascent as it is, bolsters this circumstantial evidence. For one, Hufe et al. (2018) demonstrate that economic outcomes in the US, at least, have in recent decades come to depend more on a person's circumstances of birth. They decompose the US income distribution in each year into an "unfair" component that is attributable to demographic characteristics like race, gender, parental income, and parental occupation; and a remaining "fair" portion that can be explained by differences in individual value creation. The authors find that while the expansion of income inequality was mostly fair until the 1990s, thereafter it became predominantly unfair. The entire distribution of US economic outcomes has become increasingly dependent on the circumstances of one's birth – a clear violation of economic fairness.

Second, economic unfairness has been directly linked to political upheaval. Guriev (2017) examines the political salience of unfair economic outcomes in post-Soviet states. Like Hufe et al. (2018), he sorts out the differences between *unfair* inequality that is explained by demographic characteristics (like parental education, gender, ethnicity, and place of birth) and *fair* inequality that is explained by individual merit. Unsurprisingly, Guriev finds that the unfair type of inequality is associated with lower support for democracy and the market system. Interestingly, he also finds that after controlling for *unfair* inequality, *fair* inequality is associated with slightly higher support for democracy and markets. Not only do people tie unfair outcomes to a broken social system; they have greater faith in a system when merit is more highly rewarded. Guriev (2018) explains that this finding is especially plausible in the context of post-Soviet states, which for a long time had to deal with, in his words, enforced "unfair equality."

Although this evidence is thought-provoking, it is indirect. It grapples with the nature of economic fairness and populism, and, while it poses possible links between the two, it is not systematic. This chapter will complete the argument by exploring the relationship between economic unfairness and populism in more depth. First, it will detail the correlation between low social mobility – an important type of economic unfairness – and the geography of populism. Next it will place that evidence among all the other arguments examined so far to show that economic unfairness is the *necessary* condition for contemporary populism. Finally, it will explain the rise of populism through the lens of fairness.

The Empirics of Economic Unfairness and Populism

Protzer (2019) directly assesses the relationship between economic unfairness and developed-world populism using data on social mobility. Intuitively, social mobility measures the extent to which each citizen's income depends on how wealthy their parents were. In an environment of low social mobility, it is very difficult to get ahead if you do not already come from a well-off family – a situation that clearly violates fairness. Conversely, in places with high social mobility, each person's income is not strongly influenced by how much their parents earned. Individual success depends a great deal more on individual merit, and outcomes are broadly fairer. While social mobility focuses on income across generations and does not explicitly account for factors like race, parental occupation, or place of birth, it does capture one systemically important type of economic unfairness. What's more, the available data on social mobility has reasonably good coverage, which enables comparison with populist voting patterns.

There are several reasons why, prima facie, someone might think that it is not useful to relate social mobility to patterns of populism. Perhaps the most important objection to address is the serious misperception, both popular and academic, that social mobility and income inequality are tightly interchangeable – and that the social mobility angle thus offers no new insight. Some interpret the Great Gatsby Curve from Corak (2013) in this manner, which shows that high income inequality is correlated with low social mobility across thirteen OECD countries. Bénabou (2018) details several convincing ways in which high income inequality could contribute to low social mobility. First, a number of public goods, like schools and hospitals, tend to be provided in particular geographies. If different neighborhoods have unequal levels of wealth, it may be that some provide better public services than others. Thus the rich may receive higher-quality education than the poor, stifling social mobility. Second, an affluent elite may use their wealth to influence politics in favor of their children. Third, greater inequality may lead to reductions in empathy among the affluent and, by extension, less political support for policies that facilitate social mobility. Fourth, high inequality may make society believe that those outcomes are natural and deserved, and thus that there is no rational need to invest in policies to create social mobility.

These channels almost certainly exist, and there is good evidence to suggest that income inequality does shape social mobility in some limited ways. But critically, all the evidence is that its impact is *not* decisive and that income inequality is just one of *many* factors that influence social mobility. Both in the original Great Gatsby Curve and in an alternative version where Connolly et al. (2019) examine US and Canadian local labor markets, correlations are accompanied by a large amount of unexplained dispersion. Even more crucially, Chetty and Hendren (2018) provide causal evidence showing that unequal outcomes are only loosely linked to low social mobility. In ground-breaking research, they analyze family relocation in the US to tease out the factors which lead some local labor markets to have higher social mobility than others. Income inequality affects social mobility, but *seven* other county-level variables also affect it with comparable strength – social capital, commuting time, racial segregation, racial composition (presumably reflecting discrimination), the ubiquity of single parenthood, test scores reflecting the quality of education, and the number of colleges per capita. Even then, a substantial percentage of the variation in social mobility cannot be explained by the variables available to them.

It is thus *completely* indefensible to suggest that one can simply swap out social mobility for income inequality. The two variables affect each other to be sure, but are not identical, much as one might imagine education levels and GDP per capita influence each other but are in no sense of the word interchangeable. As emphasized by Angus Deaton in the quote that leads this chapter, inequality and unfairness are not one and the same thing.

Some might also contend that social mobility is a slow-moving variable that has not changed enough to explain the rise of populism. This position is disputed but is, in principle, defensible. On the one hand, Carr and Wiemers (2016) find that the likelihood of someone moving from the middle to the top of the US income distribution has declined since the 1980s, and Hufe et al. (2018) find that parental economic status has become a far more decisive determinant of a person's earnings in the US since the 1970s. In contrast Hertz (2007), Lee and Solon (2009), and Chetty et al. (2014) conclude that American social mobility has not changed substantially over a similar time period.

The critique that social mobility has not changed enough to explain the rise of populism misses a few points. For one, social mobility is typically measured and expressed in terms of birth cohorts. So if social mobility was higher before the 1980s and then dropped, a greater share of the population would experience low social mobility with each passing year. Second, it is entirely plausible to suppose that consistently poor social mobility could lead to mounting political anger. A durable problem with no end in sight can surely lead to increasing frustration. Third, and most importantly, persistently low social mobility says a lot about the broader economic policy environment. If it is difficult to go from rags to riches across generations, it is probably also difficult to adjust to economic shocks *within* each generation. A country, state, or city with poor social mobility is arguably unlikely to handle events like the China Shock or GFC fairly. Thus there are several reasons to think that the timeline of low social mobility is compatible with the rise of populism.

Having noted these points, we can now turn to statistical analysis. As outlined in Chapter 1, we consider four contexts using multivariate regression: the 2016 and 2020 US presidential elections, the second round of the 2017 French presidential election, the 2019 European Parliament election, and surveyed confidence in national government from 2015 to 2019 across the developed world. We explore the relationship between patterns of populism and social mobility in addition to the variables described in Chapter 1 that are unrelated to economic fairness – income and wealth inequality, the presence of immigrants, the presence of older generations, and social media use.

After taking other plausibly important "control" factors into account (such as a country's income level and population size, or a US county's ethnic composition and population density), low social mobility is consistently statistically significantly correlated with the incidence of populism. Importantly, it remains statistically significant even after introducing any of the competing hypotheses for populism.

The US is an especially interesting case because its elections, over time, tell a story about the impact of economic unfairness. For the 2016 election, we control for each county's income per capita, its population density, the share of its population that is ethnically white, the share of its population that is religious, and its percent Republican presidential vote share in 2012. After taking these into account, there is a positive statistically significant correlation between the vote swing toward Trump and low social mobility. This finding also survives a series of robustness checks, the first of which involves adding in each competing hypothesis for populism one at a time. Introducing the Gini coefficient for income inequality in each county, the share of immigrants in its population, or the share of seniors in the population, does not alter either the sign (the direction of the correlation, positive versus negative) or the statistical significance of the correlation between social mobility and the vote swing toward Trump. This result additionally remains true if we measure the vote swing in relative rather than absolute terms (for example, treating a change in the Republican vote share from 10 to 15 percent as a 50 percent gain rather than a 5 percent gain).

The results for 2020 (which use the same specification, but with the added control variable of COVID-19 deaths per capita in each county up to the election date) are comparable, but with an important difference. Low social mobility is likewise positively and statistically significantly correlated with the vote swing toward Trump in 2020 versus 2012. However, the magnitude of the correlation is approximately a third of that observed in 2016. This finding is compatible with the notion that Trump may have retained some support in counties with low social mobility, but that after four years and a pandemic the strength of that following subsided somewhat – perhaps contributing to his defeat. As before, we run robustness checks on this correlation. Adding in the competing hypotheses for populism does not change the sign or the significance of the correlation between low social mobility and the vote swing, but expressing the vote swing in relative rather than absolute terms renders it statistically insignificant. Of course, there is an argument that treating a change in the Republican vote share from 10 to 15 percent as a 50 percent change is less appropriate than treating it as a 5 percent change, which is why this is a robustness check rather than the main analysis. Nevertheless this result lends credence to the idea that Trump's grip over counties that experienced economic unfairness had weakened by 2020.

In a sanity check we additionally analyze Mitt Romney's 2012 presidential run. Romney was obviously not a populist like Trump; indeed, he was known as the "Massachusetts moderate." We should expect that votes for Romney were less strongly associated with the economic unfairness of low social mobility, because he did not campaign by targeting those issues. Fascinatingly, that is exactly what the results suggest. Taking the same control variables used for the 2016 election into account, the county-level vote swing toward Romney in 2012 versus 2008 had a *negative* statistically significant relationship with social mobility. This reinforces the contention that it was not simply the Republican Party that attracted support from places that have experienced economic unfairness – it was Trump's brand of populism in particular.

The data for the French 2017 presidential election is somewhat more limited, and thus should be understood to be suggestive rather than definitive. We only analyze the French departments that are large enough to yield good social mobility data, and French policy on data that the state can legally collect makes certain demographic controls hard to come by. Nevertheless, the results are consistent with a relationship between low social mobility and populism. Controlling for each department's income per capita and population density, there is a positive statistically significant correlation between low social mobility and the vote share for Le Pen. This finding survives robustness checks where we add in the alternative hypotheses of income inequality and immigration (measured by the share of births to at least one parent of immigrant origin) one at a time.

The same association between low social mobility and populism plays out in the 2019 European Parliament elections. After controlling for each country's population and income per capita, low social mobility has a statistically significant positive correlation with the vote share for populist and far-right parties. Similar results emerge from a battery of robustness tests. First, we add in the alternative hypotheses of income inequality, the share of immigrants in the population, the share of seniors in the population, and the rate of social media use, one at a time. In each case low social mobility retains its sign and statistical significance. Second, we show that social mobility still has a positive and marginally significant correlation with votes for populist parties alone, not including non-populist far-right parties. Third, we show that social mobility has a statistically significant positive correlation if, where possible, we swap out the data source for intergenerational income elasticity (the technical term for the most commonly used metric of social mobility). Finally, social mobility is still statistically significant with the expected sign if we only examine wealthy countries with GDP per capita levels of at least $35,000.

Last, but not least, we consider confidence in national government in countries across the developed world. Worse social mobility, controlling for population and income per capita, is statistically significantly correlated with lower confidence in government. As before, we check the robustness of this finding by adding in alternative hypotheses for populism – in this case income inequality, the share of immigrants in the population, the share of seniors in the population, and the rate of social media use – one at a time. In each case, social mobility retains its sign and statistical significance. In another check we only analyze countries with GDP per capita levels of at least $35,000, in which case this correlation maintains its sign and is marginally statistically significant. Alternatively, if we swap out the intergenerational income elasticity data, Switzerland becomes a statistical outlier; when it is removed, the relationship retains its sign and significance.

All these statistical results are highly consistent, far more so than those for the alternative hypotheses examined in Chapter 1. In each instance, low social mobility is correlated with patterns of populism even after introducing competing explanations, and this is true across a variety of international and subnational contexts. A critical conclusion follows. Low social mobility, an important metric of economic unfairness, is *system-*

atically associated with the international geography of contemporary developed-world populism. The scapegoats laid out in Chapter 1, conversely, are not.

The Evidence in Summary

Recall the criteria set out in Chapter 1 for evaluating theories for populism: they ought to match its *why*, its *where*, and its *when*. We have now, finally, brought enough evidence forward to enable us to evaluate economic fairness along these lines.

First, consider the *why*, which demands that any explanation should have a feasible theoretical connection to populist discontent. As Chapter 2 explained, economic fairness is a central concern for the bulk of citizens in modern market democracies. Biological evolution gave human beings a fairness instinct, and cultural evolution has promoted fairness above other competing values in the developed world because it critically enables complex cooperation. Unlike some of the other explanations for populism, such as unequal outcomes, we should expect citizens across the developed world to be genuinely sensitive to fairness and its violation.

Additionally, populist language is couched in terms of unfairness by virtue of its moral framing. Modern definitions of populism in the academic literature agree that it is anti-elite and anti-pluralist. This entails substantial frustration with elites who allegedly rig society in their favor. That is why slogans like Trump's "Make America Great Again," Le Pen's "Au Nom du Peuple," the Leave campaign's "Take Back Control," and Geert Wilders's "Make the Netherlands Ours Again" have been so effective, and why populist figures talk about "forgotten people" in a "rigged system."

81

Economic Unfairness and the Rise of Populism

Economic unfairness has also been repeatedly linked to political discontent in academic research. Financial crises lead to support for extremist parties, but regular macroeconomic disasters of the same magnitude do not, because people care not just about the size of a loss but about how unfair it was. Job losses from trade, similarly, only represent one relatively minor part of labor market churn but are highly politically salient because it is unfair to lose your job to somebody who doesn't play by the same rules.

It is thus overwhelmingly plausible that economic unfairness could theoretically lead to populism. Citizens of the developed world are sensitive to unfairness, populists complain about unfairness, and unfairness has been associated with political upheaval in a variety of ways.

As was just demonstrated, economic unfairness is also compatible with the *where* of populism. Low social mobility correlates with the geography of populism in the US, Europe, and the developed world broadly. Importantly, this pattern holds even among countries that are not considered classically Western. Our regression analysis includes a number of East European countries, for one. What's more, existing research shows that post-Soviet countries with income distributions that are unfairly determined by demographic characteristics enjoy less support for market democracy, whereas fairly rewarding individual merit may actually increase that support.

The *when* of populism, finally, likewise matches economic unfairness. Economic outcomes have come to depend more on demographic characteristics, in the US at least, over the past several decades. While social mobility is a slow-moving variable, it reflects persistent regimes of unfairness in the countries and regions affected by populism.

The logical conclusion from this evidence is that economic unfairness is the most compelling general purpose explanation for the populist wave. The core problem is neither racism, nor wealth envy, nor cultural isolation – it is the lived reality that no matter what you do, you and your children can't get ahead because the rules are stacked to favor other people. Populist leaders have succeeded at the ballot box because they connect with people who feel that they haven't been given a fair chance at success, and that their political voices have been scorned and ignored. Today populist leaders have given these voters a chance to rebel against a society that is predisposed to keep them in their place regardless of their actual or potential capacity to create value.

How Fairness was Forgotten

Having made this point, it is important to trace the entire causal chain leading to populism through the lens of fairness. By mechanically understanding each step along the way, it may be possible to ascertain how policymakers could create better outcomes. To begin, one might ask why certain developed-world policy regimes have been especially susceptible to economic unfairness. A strong contributor, arguably, is the dominance of modes of economic thought which focus on the absolute or relative magnitude of final outcomes. This way of thinking is largely oblivious to complex moral questions of whether each individual's economic outcomes are fairly deserved.

Early political economists, like Adam Smith in *The Theory of Moral Sentiments* (2010 [1759]), put moral questions at the center of their thinking. At the time there was, in fact, no discipline called "economics." Instead, theory and argument about societal wealth appeared within the domain of "political economy," a framing that entails a broader view of society. Yet beginning in the late nineteenth century, economic theory began to coalesce around a view which largely sidelined sophisticated moral questions. The "economic man" (*homo economicus*), which spun out of the work of scholars like David Ricardo and John Stuart Mill, is a model of human behavior that emphasizes each individual's drive to maximize their own resources while minimizing the cost of doing so. This simplified, ultra-utilitarian model of reality allowed subsequent thinkers like William Jevons, Léon Walras, and Wilfredo Pareto to make great analytical advances. But at the end of the day, in this view of the world, there isn't much to say about the full spectrum of morality.

A number of prominent economists, such as John Maynard Keynes and Amartya Sen, have criticized *homo economicus* on the grounds that it provides an unrealistically super-rational model of human behavior. In practice, people are not, of course, "optimization machines" that solely and ruthlessly maximize wealth. Practical economic prediction often requires an appreciation for our irrational psychology, which Keynes famously termed our "animal spirits."

Economic theory has in some part adjusted to this critique. Herbert Simon introduced the concept of bounded rationality – that people are partly irrational due to the computational limits of our cognition. We use mental shortcuts to make decisions, and often do so based on incomplete information. Behavioral economics, in turn, is a relatively recent approach to modeling economic behavior which tries to empirically map out our preferences and mental shortcuts.

On the whole, however, *homo economicus* remains critically important to economic thought. Its use was vigorously cemented and justified by Milton Friedman in "The Methodology of Positive Economics" (1953). Friedman forcefully argued that economic theories should be judged by their predictive power, and that the realism of a theory's assumptions does not matter. According to this perspective, *homo economicus* is a useful simplification which brings enormous analytical power; the fact that it does not realistically depict human behavior is inconsequential as long as it predicts outcomes accurately. As discussed in Chapter 2, Friedman also contended that economists should not address normative, moral questions of what society *ought* to do. Instead, they should solely explore "positive" questions which describe *how* the economy works, and leave normative decisions to policymakers. *Homo economicus* is, in this view, appropriate because it abstracts from the moral questions which economists ought not to concern themselves with.

In practice, the work and advice of economists, and the lens of *homo economicus*, has come to profoundly influence public policy over the past forty years. Politicians like Ronald Reagan and Margaret Thatcher, as well as two generations of policymakers that followed, drew the simple conclusion that not only was the "market always right" but that "government is not the solution to our problem, government is the problem" and "there is no such thing as society." Economists and many policymakers came to frequently work on the assumption that greater aggregate societal wealth is always good and ought to be focused on (a classic example is how Tony Blair and Gordon Brown's New Labour were captured by this point of view). The Washington Consensus of neoliberal thought especially embraced

85

that perspective, pushing the idea of unbridled free markets as a fantastic tool for wealth accumulation, the advancement of society, and the spread of democracy. The gamut of theoretical tools which *homo economicus* enables provide the intellectual backbone of this school of thought.

In and of itself, it is by no stretch of the imagination a bad thing that *homo economicus* has been used to develop the intellectual tools that can help maximize a society's wealth. We live in a historical era with unprecedented freedom from poverty, which has been greatly enabled by the large-scale accumulation of wealth, facilitated in part by the knowledge of economics. But since the early years of the twenty-first century, there has been a growing recognition that this perspective is incomplete, and that its dogged use has blinded policymakers to other important concerns – which now risks undoing an important part of the progress that has been made.

The GFC and its aftermath, for one, resulted in the castigation of certain forms of wealth accumulation as extremely high risk and disproportionately dangerous to the most vulnerable members of society. It has also highlighted the way *homo economicus*, despite Friedman's exhortations, limits our predictive power. In November 2008, Queen Elizabeth II famously put the question to economists about the crisis: "Why did no one see it coming?" The rise of populism further enforced the idea that standard economic prescriptions, such as free trade, implemented without appropriate public support for citizens to adjust, can be very harmful to some segments of society. Phenomena like these have led some economists to chart a new course and take normative, moral questions much more seriously.

Such a rethink is rightly deserved. *Homo economicus* has produced useful theory, but it has left the economic profession – and the political schools of thought that embrace neoliberalism – ill-equipped to think about fairness. If an analytical framework can only maximize output, it is inherently blind to all but the most utilitarian moral questions. As has been repeatedly argued, different paths to the same change in net societal wealth in fact can vary dramatically in how fair they are. Yet an economic theory that exclusively focuses on wealth maximization has no tools with which to even consider this kind of distinction.

While one critique of *homo economicus* is that we are, in reality, irrational, a deeper and arguably more important one is that we are *social*. We are not static utility maximizers, but strategic, game-theoretical agents who are most productive when we work together on a massive scale. As outlined, humans evolved to value fairness in order to optimize stable and productive cooperation. When a democratic society ceases to be organized according to rules that most people consider fair, those rules will be voted out or overthrown – with the risk that they could be replaced with something worse.

Unfortunately, too much of the alternative perspective that contests *homo economicus* has been framed in hard-left ideological terms that ultimately fare no better. Radical egalitarian critics of modern capitalism focus on unequal outcomes and ignore whether the reasons for those outcomes are in fact fair. Instead of maximizing aggregate societal output, they argue that relative differences in output per person should be dramatically minimized. The policy prescriptions associated with this simplistic approach are not only off the mark but severely counterproductive, because enforced equal outcomes have proven time and time again to create catastrophically unfair societies. As Jonathan Freedland (2020) has noted, for example, polling in the UK confirms that:

[M]any of the voters that Labour needs to win associate "equality" with levelling down. They think it means everyone is getting the same, no matter how hard they work. Those voters don't like that notion, believing it robs them of the opportunity to get on . . . They reckon your actions should have consequences, that if you work hard you deserve to be rewarded. For them, "equality" contradicts that. More effective is "fairness," and the insistence that everyone deserves a fair shot.

These alternative strains of simplified, ideological economic thought are two sides of the same coin, and both have contributed to the rise of populism on a deep level over the past half-century. The political right, particularly since the Reagan/Thatcher revolution of the 1980s, has challenged the role of the state in many questionable ways in order to maximize GDP. The political left, especially since the postwar propagation of Soviet ideas, has aimed to aggressively redistribute economic success. Both approaches are blind to fairness. The results can be observed, for example, in France's statist, redistributionist instincts or in America's penchant for market solutions to every societal problem. Low social mobility pervades in both nations, and both have proven susceptible to illiberal populism.

The full gamut of policy inputs to economic fairness, and the particular ways key countries have failed on them, will be addressed in detail in Chapters 4 and 5. For the moment, it is important to simply note the consequences of these shortcomings. On the one hand, simplistic neoliberal and quasi-Marxist policy instincts have led to *intergenerational* unfairness – the way circumstances of birth can limit someone's life chances – in affected countries. This sort of unfairness is captured by low social mobility, but also pertains to the way geography, social strata, race, and more can hold a citizen back. One can only imagine the resentment that builds when an individual's life trajectory is sharply constrained by the social and economic position of the family they are born into, whether as a result of discrimination, insufficient access to public goods, or an overbearing state that regulates and taxes away chances of success.

It is equally important, however, to emphasize aspects of *intragenerational* unfairness that result from the same pool of policy failures. These types of problems expose citizens to uncontrollable shocks in a way that unfairly cuts them off from future opportunity. Some of these issues are relatively latent. For example, insufficient access to affordable healthcare can, in the event of illness, easily result in bankruptcy regardless of a citizen's capacity for future productivity. This problem has, perhaps unsurprisingly, featured strongly in US elections in recent years. A stagnant economy that does not embrace value creation, by the same token, makes it exceedingly difficult to bounce back from cyclical job loss or business closure.

Perhaps more dramatic contributors to intragenerational unfairness are the types of acute society-wide shocks discussed in Chapter 1. American policymakers must closely consider why there was no evidence of job recovery in the US following the China Shock, but some 60 percent of affected Canadians found alternative work. There is also a question of whether the advent of automation technology has been handled well by certain countries. Acemoglu and Restrepo (2020) show that one additional industrial robot per thousand workers in US labor markets reduces the employment rate by 0.2 percent and wage earnings by 0.42 percent. Autor (2019) discusses how technological change has undermined demand for labor that performs medium-skill routine tasks, contributing to stagnant wages for non-college-educated US men. The GFC and the policy response to it likewise created enormous upheaval for many citizens across the world, and the COVID-19 pandemic has disrupted labor markets on an almost unprecedented scale. Even the fairest and most socially mobile countries have been seriously challenged by all these events. The least fair have been badly unprepared. A job loss is made all the more difficult when a frayed social safety net fails to smooth the shock or help a worker adjust, and when moribund markets offer scant alternative opportunities.

As grievances from both intergenerational and intragenerational economic unfairness mounted, many affected citizens sought third parties to blame – and thereby amplified its political consequences. The results can be observed in the inflammatory, culturally divisive identity politics that go hand-in-hand with populism the world over. For instance, Enke (2020) documents how, from 2008 to 2018, Americans came to hold values that were more communal than universal, such as emphasizing in-group loyalty ahead of protecting the disadvantaged throughout society. What's more, he shows that these communal values were associated with the 2016 vote swing toward Trump.

Some commentators argue that the frequent right-wing cultural-political tilt of populism is inexplicably irrational, because the same struggling citizens who support it would purportedly benefit from a larger state provided instead by the left. Actually, Alesina, Stantcheva, and Teso (2018) demonstrate that citizens across the developed world with right-wing beliefs and low trust in government do not see redistribution as a good solution for low social mobility. The redistributionist perspective fails to recognize that populist anger over economic unfairness is not merely a cool-headed financial calculation. As Fukuyama (2018) points out, "economic grievances become much more acute when they are attached to feelings of indignity and disrespect." Populist discontent in fact derives from the sense that you, your family, and your community have been denied a fair chance to succeed by the powers that be, and is therefore intensely political. However flawed, the all-too-human response is to protect one's family and community against untrustworthy or adversarial outsiders. Right-wing populists often speak in terms that emphasize this in-group loyalty, which is an important reason why they have succeeded at the ballot box.

Given this predilection, it should be unsurprising that populist discontent has frequently connected with underlying societal frictions, real and imagined. Alesina, Miano, and Stantcheva (2018), for example, show that right-wing respondents without a college education (a key demographic for would-be populist voters) in multiple developed countries are significantly likelier than other citizens to believe that immigrants are unemployed and uneducated. By implication, immigrants are perceived to be both a source of blue-collar labor market competition and a drain on public coffers. As one might recall from quotes earlier in this book, a sense of betrayal results – that distant elites support foreign "others" instead and at the expense of the "true people."

The spillover of populist grievances into the cultural domain hardly stops there. Social and digital media arguably magnifies these fractures, splitting society into tribes that demonize rather than try to understand each other. Much of the internet inflicts a daily deluge of insults and disdain on would-be populist voters, sometimes including prestigious news outlets (seen in op-eds with titles like "Trump's Army of Angry White

Men," which featured in the *New York Times* in 2020). Condescension thus complements the experience of economic unfairness, and reinforces the perspective that unfairness results from the malign actions of adversarial elites and out-groups. Exogenous cultural factors like immigration and social media cannot, as repeatedly emphasized, systematically explain the populist wave. But where economic unfairness persists, its political ramifications have unfolded by inflaming cultural conflict.

While populism has exploded in countries that struggle with economic unfairness, those which are comparatively fair have proven to possess apparent firewalls that limit – if not wholly eliminate – its impact. In Canada, for example, the populist People's Party totally failed to connect with any salient issue in the 2019 federal election and received less than 2 percent of the national vote (albeit partly because of Canada's first-past-the-post voting system). Another crucial example can be found in Nordic countries with high social mobility that experienced non-negligible disruptions in the form of the 2015 European migrant crisis. Recall from Chapter 1 that the share of immigrants in the populations of the UK, Italy, and France are in the range of 10–16 percent. These countries also voted for populist parties in the 2019 European Parliament election at very high rates of approximately 30–50 percent. Given that Nordic countries experienced unusually high migration inflows during the crisis, and that in 2019 Denmark and Sweden were 13 percent and 20 percent foreign-born, one might have expected similarly large support for populism. Yet that widespread support did not materialize, and did not lead to major institutional disruption.

There was most certainly the appearance of a rising populist threat. Whereas the Sweden Democrats won no seats in either national or European Parliament elections from 1988 to 2009, for instance, they received nearly 13 percent of the vote in the 2014 national election. In the run-up to the 2018 general election, many commentators forecasted major electoral gains. The Sweden Democrats and the neighboring Danish People's Party are credited with shifting policy positions more decisively against multiculturalism and mass immigration among mainstream parties. The purely cultural backlash against the migrant crisis was, in a sense, thus very real.

But when push came to shove, Nordic populists did not overrun their respective homelands. After capturing 21 percent of the vote share in the 2015 national election, the Danish People's Party deflated to 9 percent in 2019. The Sweden Democrats improved on their earlier results to receive 18 percent of the vote in the 2018 national election, and Denmark and Sweden respectively voted for populists at rates of 11 percent and 15 percent in the 2019 European Parliament election. Yet while these kinds of results are tangible, they did not touch the rates of support for populism seen elsewhere in Europe and did not create comparable consequences. They did not even meet the average vote share for populists among all countries in the 2019 European Parliament election, at approximately 23 percent.

The constrained impact of populism in Nordic countries after the migrant crisis resulted, in part, from the empathetic response of the political mainstream. Rather than label voters concerned about excessive immigration as somehow racist, numerous mainstream parties pivoted toward supporting reduced migration in a way that was still compatible with liberal democracy. The Swedish Social Democrats (not to be confused with the Sweden Democrats), traditionally the country's ruling party, for example, advocated a very large reduction in refugee inflows. This shift is often viewed as part and parcel of populism, but it is crucial to also understand it as a fair response to legitimate concerns about cultural dislocation, which maintained the electoral viability of the liberal democratic mainstream.

However, the Nordic economies had a crucial firewall against illiberal populism, which made this kind of political strategy feasible to begin with: their high levels of social mobility are associated with an environment of economic fairness. In other parts of Europe, like Italy, France, the UK, and Eastern Germany, the migrant crisis connected to underlying economic unfairness to create the explosive perception that elites were diverting funds and attention from struggling natives to newcomers. But Nordic populists could not so easily pin down the political establishment in this way. The debate thus arguably remained more of a self-contained discussion about multiculturalism, and it was easier for mainstream parties to appear credible when they claimed to support reduced immigration and to be on the same side as regular citizens.

The divergent experiences of relatively fair versus unfair high-income countries over the past several decades prompts a number of important policy questions. If hewing too closely to neoliberal and quasi-Marxist ideologies makes a society prone to economic unfairness and thereby illiberal populism, what instead should be the intellectual pillars on which to build a fair economy and reclaim populism? If such pillars can be identified, what policy prescriptions do they concretely entail? How do those prescriptions differ from the current practices of developed countries troubled by populism, and what reforms might specific nations prioritize? The key to answering these questions, we will argue, lies in the twin virtues of equal opportunity and fair unequal outcomes.

4

The Twin Virtues of Equal Opportunity and Fair Unequal Outcomes

I think you should be able to become a billionaire and a millionaire, but pay your fair share.

President Joe Biden, April 2021

[The] American Patriots who voted for me . . . will not be disrespected or treated unfairly in any way, shape or form!!!

President Donald Trump, January 8, 2020

As argued, the conventional prescriptions of the political left and right are unlikely to resolve the challenge of populism because they do not sufficiently speak to the core issue of economic fairness. This chapter will construct a new policy framework by looking into the categories of inputs that underpin a fair economy. Importantly, our goal is not to generate a definitive, fully comprehensive list of best practices that every country should adopt. It is instead to organize thinking about the policies that support economic fairness and high social mobility, so that – as we will detail in Chapter 5 – any country can diagnose specific areas that need attention, and then execute reforms in line with their particular political, institutional, and cultural realities. We will argue that two overarching virtues form the policy basis for economic fairness: equal opportunity and fair unequal outcomes.

There is a long history of commentary regarding what constitutes equal opportunity and a fair market outcome. Many will have their own opinions surrounding these principles. To be as clear as possible on what "equal opportunity" and "fair unequal outcomes" mean in this book, we will briefly describe their key components in the abstract, explain how they work in tandem to create economic fairness, and then explore illustrative policies associated with each element at some length.

Figure 4.1 presents a diagram of the twin virtues and each of their subbranches, which we will consider one at a time. This schematic is not meant to be interpreted as a rigid hierarchy of relationships between different policies. It is simply a practical framework to categorize relevant public policy inputs, each of which work together to make economic fairness possible.

Equal opportunity requires that personal characteristics that do not intrinsically determine productivity should not hold a person back from success. It is not fair that a citizen's race, gender, or family wealth, for example, should constrain their life chances because, as detailed in Chapter 2, these types of factors do not determine ability and productivity in and of themselves. Of course, as stressed earlier, this rule does not extend to nontransferable personal characteristics that genuinely drive productivity. Natural genius, beauty, and athletic talent *must* be rewarded insofar as they make an individual more productive.

We divide equal opportunity with respect to personal characteristics into two subcategories: "formal" and "substantive." The first of these inputs, formal equal opportunity, can be understood as freedom from discrimination. It mandates that, in the broadest sense,

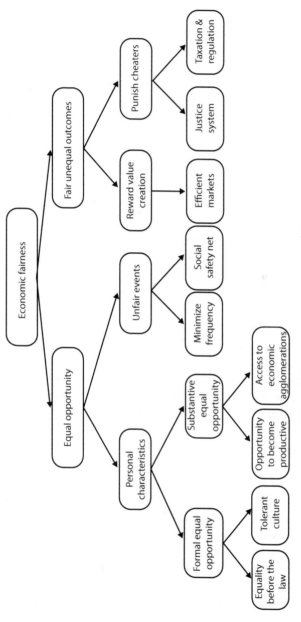

Figure 4.1: Inputs to economic fairness

the same rules of competition should apply to everyone regardless of race, gender, sexuality, accent, and other purely demographic characteristics. Two equally qualified candidates applying for a job, for example, should have the same chances of success regardless of any of these factors. This requires not only equality under the law, which illegalizes discrimination de jure, but also a tolerant culture to eliminate it de facto. It goes without saying that every liberal democracy struggles to reduce the unfairness from these types of biases, some countries more than others.

But ending discrimination through formal equal opportunity, in and of itself, does not wholly erase the influence of factors that do not intrinsically drive productivity. Of course, someone from a wealthy family will usually have far better access to education (including schools, contacts, tutors, laptops, and materials) than someone from a middle- or working-class family, and thus have a much greater chance of economic success. That is why *substantive* equal opportunity is also needed, which necessitates that all citizens have a real chance both to become productive and to access economic opportunities. The former of these goals entails inputs like childcare, childhood nutrition, and high-quality education, which allow citizens to cultivate their abilities and ultimately become competitive in the labor market. The latter goal recognizes that even if citizens can hone their skills, they must then be able to personally connect with good career opportunities that are overwhelmingly located in urban centers. Inputs like affordable access to public transportation, housing, and digital communications are therefore crucial.

Yet personal characteristics are not the only potential barrier to unequal opportunity. Unfair events can disrupt a person's livelihood and abruptly cut them off from future success, like a financial crisis that forces their family business to close or a car accident that lands them with a potentially enormous medical bill. On the one hand, the state has a duty to minimize the frequency and severity of unfair events like wars, pandemics, and financial crises. This requires active regulation and astute leadership. At the same time, however, many forms of personal tragedies such as ill-health or an abrupt layoff are, to a large extent, unavoidable. The state must thus ensure that unfair events, even if they occur, do not destroy a citizen's prospects of future opportunity. A social safety net, consisting of inputs like universal healthcare, unemployment insurance, and retraining, is necessary to smooth over unfair shocks.

Perhaps unsurprisingly, equal opportunity on the whole thus implies a significant role for the state. In a laissez-faire society, disparities in parental wealth mean that some naturally gifted citizens will not be able to afford education, private transport, or housing in city centers, and can be bankrupted by an unexpected layoff or illness. They may not be able to fully cultivate their talents, access the job market, or bounce back from tragedy, and the prospect of economic success is very limited. The only practical solution is for the state to regulate private markets and create public goods to bridge these gaps.

These efforts can be juxtaposed with another form of state intervention that should be thought of very differently: aggressive redistribution. It is one thing to create progressive taxation and sponsor a basic safety net, which can fairly and effectively support equal opportunity. It is another thing entirely to punitively cut down the most prosperous members of society and transfer wealth from the rich to the poor en masse for the sake of equalization itself. Doing so creates radically different (usually worse) economic incentives and, moreover, can fail to create the tangible goods – like widely available education and public transit – that open up obvious and workable paths to success. Substantive equal opportunity requires a state that actively creates equal opportunity, but not one that punishes success.

That being said, it is critical to stress that economic fairness is not purely the result of state intervention because fair unequal outcomes achieved through the market are just as important as equal opportunity. A fair economy must reward the activities that create surpluses without infringing on the productivity of others. Part of this entails that society must embrace rewarding value creation, which requires an efficient market economy – and, in turn, a greatly varied range of policies that are conventionally understood as contributors to economic growth. This book makes absolutely no pretense to explain the forces behind economic growth in detail, but one might think of obvious inputs like macroeconomic stability, high-quality infrastructure, anti-monopoly laws, nonpunitive taxation, and many more.

At the same time, society must punish rather than reward "cheaters" who attempt to get ahead at the expense of others. An effective justice system must prevent outright criminality that directly harms others, such as corruption, nepotism, and theft. Regulation and taxation must also be designed to disincentivize economic strategies that indirectly impose costs on others, such as monopoly, high-risk financial activities, wage suppression, pollution, and unsafe business practices.

These measures against "cheaters" additionally imply that the political system must be inoculated against interference from economic elites. One school of thought, as discussed in Chapter 1, is that populism results from overpowerful elites who bend political rules to their benefit, and the appropriate response is to expropriate the assets of those elites. We would argue, however, that such expropriation is only necessary in the most extreme situations where elites are so powerful that they can simply override institutional safeguards – think perhaps of colonial-era Latin America. Many contemporary market democracies instead get by through careful regulation, which is fairer because it does not punish success. It is worth remembering, for instance, that Swedish billionaires hold wealth equivalent to a larger share of GDP than American billionaires. If American policymaking is more subject to the influence of the wealthy, it is not because they are proportionally richer but because the US has failed to rein in lax lobbying and campaign finance practices.

Critically, economic fairness can only be achieved when these twin virtues – which are two sides of the same coin – are jointly satisfied. On the one hand, a system where both opportunity and outcomes are *equal* is unfair because it totally fails to reward value creation. At the same time, a society wherein both opportunity and outcomes are *unequal* is unfair because citizens are held back by factors that do not intrinsically determine productivity. While the former of these two arrangements corresponds to communism and the latter to laissez-faire neoliberalism, both result in unfairness. Only with *equal* opportunity and *fair unequal* outcomes can economic rewards largely be decided by contribution, and fairness is then possible. What's more, these twin virtues are mutually reinforcing. The market is more efficient under equal opportunity because society can most effectively utilize everybody's talents, and funding the public goods that undergird equal opportunity requires the surpluses created by fair unequal market outcomes.

Having established this basic framework, let us consider a sample of the policies each branch might require in somewhat more detail. As stated, the point here is to stimulate intuition with some notable examples and not to provide an exhaustive list. We will go through the branches depicted above in Figure 4.1 in the following five sections, and do so in approximately the chronological order of when they impact a person's life – so that in sum one can imagine how they work together to create fairness and social mobility. First, the chapter will examine substantive equal opportunity. It will study how education policy shapes a citizen's ability to become productive, and then how access to public transportation and affordable housing impact their capacity to access the labor market. Second, it will consider formal equal opportunity with special attention to the prominent contemporary question of how to handle culturally ingrained discrimination. Third, it will assess equal opportunity with respect to unfair events, and specifically delve into health and unemployment policy. Fourth, it will probe how markets create and reward value. We will abstract from the enormous literature on economic growth and home in on counterproductive policies that expressly punish success. Finally, the chapter will inspect several key inputs to punishing economic "cheaters" – financial regulation, comparative taxation of labor versus capital income, and antitrust.

Substantive Equal Opportunity

Perhaps the most obvious and widely agreed-upon policy input that gives everyone the chance to become productive is education. There are enormous differences among high-income countries in the extent to which a citizen's socioeconomic background unfairly influences both the level of their educational attainment and the quality of their learning. Figure 4.2 shows the rate of university education among young adults whose parents only achieved high school or vocational education by country. Figure 4.3 displays how a one standard deviation increase in socioeconomic status (as measured by the Program for International Student Assessment – PISA) influences math scores in selected OECD countries.

In some respects this data is unsurprising. Most countries that perform well invest heavily in education, such as Canada and several North European nations. Conversely, certain South and East European countries have especially unfair educational outcomes that are strongly determined by family origins. Perhaps more interesting and important is the fact that some countries that make tertiary education very inexpensive actually do not perform well on one or both of these measures. Socioeconomic differences strongly influence PISA scores in France and Belgium, while Austria, Germany, and Italy suffer from low intergenerational educational mobility.

A key takeaway from these patterns is that reducing cost barriers for students is plausibly a necessary but not a sufficient condition for an education system that bolsters equal opportunity. On the one hand, high privately borne university tuition can be a clear barrier to equal opportunity, as manifested in countries like the US where average student debt runs into the tens of thousands of dollars. This kind of debt not only discourages access to education but, if incurred, hampers future spending on other essential goods for equal opportunity, such as housing. Significant public subsidies – at the very least for those who cannot otherwise afford university fees – are arguably necessary. Yet countries

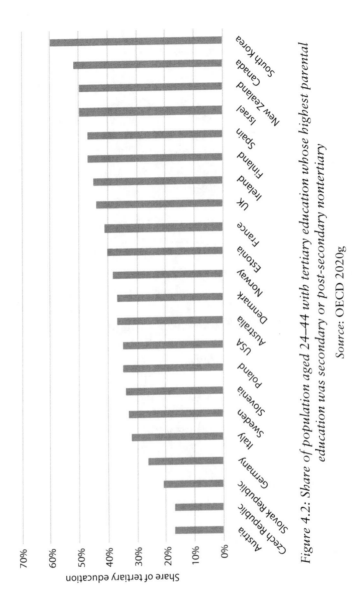

Figure 4.2: *Share of population aged 24–44 with tertiary education whose highest parental education was secondary or post-secondary nontertiary*

Source: OECD 2020g

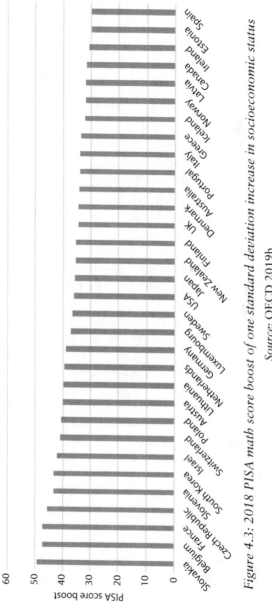

Figure 4.3: 2018 PISA math score boost of one standard deviation increase in socioeconomic status
Source: OECD 2019b

like Canada and New Zealand prove that university tuition need not be completely free to provide good educational outcomes; and given how they outperform countries with cheaper tuition in some instances, they suggest that best practices across every stage of education also matter.

There is a very wide literature on education policy which advocates for any number of best practices. Some such practices that pertain to the efficacy and fairness of primary and secondary education are summarized by the OECD (Schleicher 2020). For example, the degree to which society and policy values the teaching profession is directly connected to the quality of teaching in a country. In countries such as Malaysia, Singapore, South Korea, and Finland, more than 60 percent of teachers agree that the teaching profession is valued by society; in contrast, fewer than 10 percent agree in France, Sweden, and Spain.

Teacher compensation is one straightforward input to society's valuation of the teaching profession. While in some countries teaching is a low-paying job that does not attract the best and the brightest, in others, like Finland and Singapore, teachers are paid very well and, as a result, high-quality candidates are attracted to the profession. In combination with raising salaries, these countries also make entry to the teaching profession very competitive. For instance, there are usually at least nine applicants for each place in Finnish teacher education courses. Other factors include the autonomy teachers have in their teaching methods and the amount of creative design that goes into their practices. All this adds up to a high degree of perceived teacher professionalism, which in turn attracts, retains, and motivates high-quality teachers who can help students reach their potential.

Equal Opportunity and Fair Unequal Outcomes

It is just as important to have rules geared toward an educational system of fairness and intergenerational mobility in which all students are expected to succeed and are not held back from possible career paths, whether vocational or academic. Students in many parts of Germany, for instance, are divided into academic and vocational tracks at the early age of 10. Underpinning this system is a long-held belief – not challenged until recently – that academic education would not benefit students from working-class families, as they would simply go on to enter working-class jobs like their parents before them. This unfair belief and practice holds back disadvantaged students from choosing their own path.

Fairer education outcomes are possible when students are not divided into different ability-based streams, but all are kept in a single stream where high achievement is universally expected. This mentality is essential to fairness because it gives every student a chance to achieve the highest degree of success at whatever they choose, rather than consigning them to predetermined outcomes. Instead of streaming, customized learning can occur insofar as the teacher modifies each student's learning strategy to meet a uniform set of high standards. Some students undoubtedly require more time and effort, or a different learning method, to absorb material that comes easily to others, and this may be especially true of those from disadvantaged backgrounds. Entire classes in disadvantaged locations may require extra attention and investment. Yet it would be deeply unfair to deny those students the opportunity for success, and with sufficient student and teacher effort, success is possible for the vast majority of pupils. The workability and fairness of this model is proven in countries like Australia and Canada, which take students from vastly diverse immigrant backgrounds into single streams and educate them to the same standard.

But even if someone can enroll in school, take the best classes available, and gain truly marketable skills, they may still not be able to access the hubs of economic opportunity that open the door to well-paying labor markets or further education. The highest-paying job opportunities, for instance, overwhelmingly exist in cities, and would-be job seekers face a number of corresponding barriers pertaining to the costs of relocation, housing, transportation, and access to digital communication. To actualize substantive equal opportunity, the state must actively and efficiently reduce these barriers. As we will touch on later, this does not mean consigning certain geographies to economic failure. Creating new economic agglomerations in left-behind regions and improving access to existing ones can be complementary.

Housing policy is an especially tricky but important input to get right. The cost of housing in many cities around the world has accelerated sharply in recent years. According to the Center on Budget and Policy Priorities, the median rent in the US increased 13 percent from 2001 – 2018 while median renters' household income only increased 0.5 percent. Whereas housing costs ate up 8 percent of US GDP in the 1970s, they now consume 11 percent. As shown in Figure 4.4, rent now accounts for a high share of disposable income – often near or above 25 percent – in many OECD countries. In several countries, as shown in Figure 4.5, a huge share of the low-income population devotes more than 40 percent of disposable income to rent. While there is some scope for public housing projects to alleviate these pressures, it may be unwise to veer too far from a private housing market. There is an important discussion to be had in how the state can make private

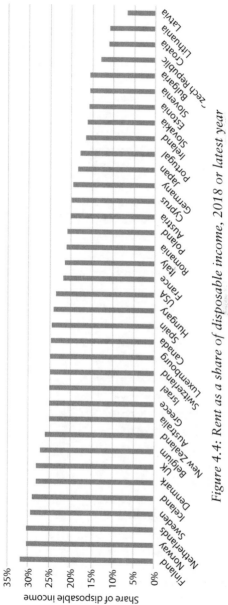

Figure 4.4: Rent as a share of disposable income, 2018 or latest year

Source: OECD 2020h

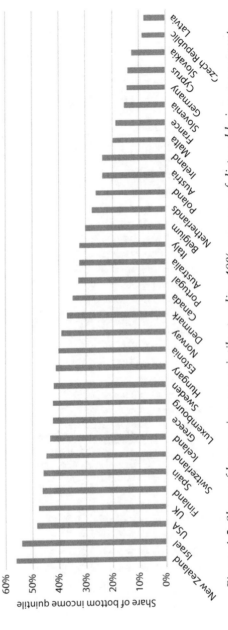

Figure 4.5: Share of bottom income quintile spending 40% or more of disposable income on rent, 2019 or latest year

Source: OECD 2020e

housing markets affordable without wholly relying on such direct intervention. In practice this often requires a complicated mix of national and local policies.

An example of an often overlooked but crucially important national-level policy is the range of interest rates set by central banks. After the 2008 financial crisis, cheap credit was sorely needed to support the economy, but many years later rock-bottom emergency interest rates still persist in many developed countries – reinforced by the COVID-19 epidemic. This has had the perverse effect of overheating some real-estate markets. In fact, Miles and Monro (2019) of the Bank of England observe that, relative to consumer goods, housing prices in the UK were roughly three and a half times higher in 2018 than they had been in 1968. They find that unexpected decreases in interest rates over recent decades could more than account for this price surge, and that a 1 percent increase in real interest rates could ultimately drive down UK housing prices by as much as 20 percent.

There was and is a missing conversation about housing market fairness in the monetary policy response to the GFC. While low interest rates were required for businesses to survive, such low rates arguably should have been treated as a strictly emergency measure and brought back up quickly as the recovery proceeded. It is not fair that housing has been made less affordable – a regressive measure that disproportionately limits the economic opportunity of the already disadvantaged – in order to maintain an extended recovery period for business and markets.

The tax incentives and regulations pertaining to local development can also strongly influence housing prices. For example, in a January 2020 special report on housing markets, *The Economist* noted that in countries such as the UK local taxes collected from real-estate development are directed to higher aggregations of government, such as national-level coffers. This means local governments often have little incentive to encourage or even permit development. An associated issue in Britain is "land-banking," where large property companies hold on to undeveloped land for an extended period of time. Restrictive regulation is a contributory factor to this problem, as companies cannot risk unpredictable planning permissions that might hold up construction start dates, and they are thus forced to apply for them in advance. So too is the lack of substantial taxation on undeveloped property, which makes this practice financially sustainable. Both issues stem from insufficient motive for local governments to obtain tax revenues from property. In Switzerland, conversely, local tax revenues from real-estate development stay local. The number of homes constructed per person each year in Switzerland is, by no coincidence, more than twice that in the UK. Housing construction can also be disincentivized by obstructive "Not In My Back Yard" planning rules that are by and large determined locally. In the 2000s, Tokyo enacted a set of reforms to streamline the real-estate development application process and allow more private determination of land use. Housing construction has since increased 30 percent.

There is more scope for direct government intervention in transportation. Even if people cannot afford to live precisely where an economic opportunity is located, effective and inexpensive public transportation can create access (and do so efficiently; the natural economies of scale exhibited in mass transit can make public solutions superior to monopolistic private alternatives). A report for the UK Department for Transport carried out by Gates et al. succinctly states that a major impact of transportation policy is "providing affordable

112

access – from people's homes to opportunities, including education, employment, family and social networks" (2019: 5).

Failing to make these kinds of investments leaves private vehicle ownership as the only viable option for citizens to access economic opportunity, but this is prohibitively expensive for most low-income families. In the US, which has one of the highest per capita vehicle ownership rates in the world and generally eschews public transit, people in the lowest income quintile devoted 16 percent of their consumption to transportation in 2019 (most of which comprised vehicle- and fuel-related expenses), according to the Bureau of Labor Statistics. This presents a sizable geographic barrier to equal opportunity; imagine how an intervention as simple as subsidized bus passes would improve the life chances of these citizens.

Many other developed countries do far better on this issue. In the European Union, people in the bottom income quintile spend approximately 7.5 percent of their earnings on transportation. Unsurprisingly, much of this discrepancy is a direct consequence of differences in public investment. The US spends roughly half as much as the EU does on transport infrastructure as a share of GDP. But specialization away from public transit also puts more cars on the road, which creates its own costs. According to the OECD, road maintenance costs per capita in 2015 were more than two and a half times higher in the US than in the UK, and more than three times higher than in France.

While intercity public transit – such as Europe's or Japan's train networks – promotes fairer access to widely dispersed economic opportunities and encourages economic development beyond leading cities, within-city urban transit connects people to opportunities in neighborhoods that they could not otherwise afford to live near (Revington and Townsend 2016). Policymakers looking to create more equal opportunity should balance the need to improve transportation within particular cities versus across regions, depending on the context.

Formal Equal Opportunity

Once citizens are given a fair chance to become productive and access economic agglomerations, the process in which they compete for opportunities ought to be free from discrimination. One can imagine that a citizen might get a good education and find an affordable apartment in an up-and-coming city, but then have the door slam shut on their future because an employer doesn't like their skin color or accent.

Almost every high-income country today largely agrees that this kind of discrimination is wrong, and has laws against it. Discriminating against someone's race or gender has been illegal for decades across the developed world, and an increasing number of nations are moving to ban discrimination on the basis of additional factors like sexuality.

Yet there is lots of evidence to suggest that demographic characteristics can still unfairly limit a person's life chances. For example, an investigation by the *Asahi Shimbun* newspaper found evidence that ten medical universities in Japan systematically tampered with their admissions in recent years to reduce the number of female entrants. An anonymous source from the prestigious Tokyo Medical University stated that the reason behind this discrimination was that "many female students who graduate end up leaving the actual medical practice to give birth and raise children." The procedural fairness that formal equal opportunity aims to provide is most seriously limited in the developed world today not by the lack of anti-discrimination legislation, but by the extent to which culture remains discriminatory.

Changing deeply held discriminatory beliefs is, of course, extremely difficult. Humans are highly pre-disposed toward confirmation bias, and generally are not receptive to being flatly told that their values are somehow evil. The brutal reality is that social progress happens through generations of thoughtful public discourse and demonstration, and by creating as much equal opportunity as possible through other means so that society is replete with examples of successful individuals from every background.

Dealing with discrimination poses an especially serious challenge in countries affected by populism, because marginalized groups are often scapegoated for systemic societal unfairness that exists for reasons wholly unrelated to them. Unfortunately, it is usually not an adequate solution to insist that scapegoating must end on its own terms regardless of broader social, political, and economic unfairness. Trump was elected, after all, in an environment of "woke" politics, where discrimination was vocally excoriated. The practical reality is that discriminatory scapegoating is an ugly element of human nature that especially tends to come out when people feel they are being treated unfairly. People are programmed to punish "cheaters" in unfair situations, and they may unfairly direct that punishment toward groups that are not truly to blame. While the act of discrimination must always be condemned, at a certain point it is pragmatic for policymakers to pay attention to the unfairness which leads people to scapegoat others for their troubles in the first place. Thus a critical element of cultivating a nondiscriminatory culture

115

is for policymakers to advance societal fairness in every respect, and thereby reduce the tension that can lead to scapegoating.

Insofar as public leaders directly address culture to reduce discrimination, they must be careful not to fall into the most pernicious forms of identity politics, which assign demographics as either "good" or "evil," like a white patriarchy. There are two major problems with this approach, the first being that it doesn't work very well. Authors such as Fukuyama (2018), Norris and Inglehart (2019), and Kaufmann (2018) discuss the resentment that identity politics breeds among those treated as immoral oppressors – especially when that treatment is applied on the basis of uncontrollable, purportedly "privileged" demographic factors. That resentment inflames rather than reduces societal tension.

The second problem is that this extreme variety of identity politics is fundamentally unfair and antithetical to equal opportunity. The entire point of ending discrimination is to create a society in which people are not punished for uncontrollable demographic characteristics such as race, gender, or sexuality. Yet strident forms of identity politics do just that by assigning moral worth to individuals based on their family origins.

In some countries it may be difficult for public leaders to avoid identity politics outright. There is always an incentive for politicians to excite their base – especially in countries where parties have internal primary election systems – which in today's polarized world can mean vilifying the types of voters who oppose them. But policymakers should bear in mind that ending discrimination is about eliminating maltreatment for the oppressed, not inventing new forms of discrimination against categories of purported oppressors.

Equal Opportunity with Respect to Unfair Events

With policy inputs in place such as those described above, citizens ought to enjoy equal opportunity with respect to their personal characteristics. But an entirely different class of problems can still prevent equal opportunity from being realized: unfair events. It is unfair if a citizen, after studying and working hard to get a well-paying job, has their future prospects derailed by a sudden shock.

We can first consider the state's role in managing the incidence of sudden, sharply unfair societal events, such as wars, financial crises, and pandemics. Of course it is in most people's interests to avoid these calamities outright, as anyone's life can be massively and unfairly affected when they occur. There is a clear onus on governments to reduce the likelihood of unfair large-scale disruptions to society.

In some cases, however, such events cannot be fully prevented and their effects must be mitigated. In these circumstances, policymakers ought not to simply examine aggregate average consequences when evaluating a possible response. The state must be attentive to the unfair way a shock can more easily destroy the livelihoods of those who are already struggling. One important reason why this occurs is that disadvantaged citizens have the least liquidity with which to privately smooth shocks. For instance, the US Federal Reserve found in 2018 that 40 percent of Americans have less than $400 in savings. If policymakers do not take such vulnerabilities into account, many disadvantaged families are liable to face immense financial disruption – with lasting unfair consequences for them and their children.

The initial policy response to the COVID-19 pandemic is a salient example. In the early months of 2020 numerous governments around the world considered "herd immunity" strategies, in which the virus would have been permitted to partly spread through the population so that enough citizens would become immune and thus stop being vectors for disease. While it soon became clear that this strategy would lead to an unacceptable number of deaths, it was also problematic given that it was deemed deeply unfair. Disadvantaged families often have inferior access to healthcare (even in countries with universal public health services), disproportionately suffer from underlying medical conditions, have fewer savings, and are more likely to work in jobs which cannot be performed from home. A herd immunity strategy (even if the COVID-19 virus had been somewhat less deadly) would have exacted especially high rates of mortality and financial distress on households that were already struggling. Undoubtedly, the sharp unfairness of this strategy was an important reason why it was quickly dropped as a possibility in most countries.

Other sorts of unfair events are not sudden, society-wide catastrophes but perennial and slow-burning personal tragedies, such as an unexpected illness or being laid off in an economic downturn. The costs associated with these events can unfairly limit a person's long-term economic opportunity, and – for the same reasons outlined above, such as insufficient access to liquidity – can carry especially severe consequences for disadvantaged households and their children. A critical role for the state is to provide a social safety net so that a person's long-term economic opportunity is not unfairly disrupted by these kinds of events.

Universal healthcare is a crucial input to fairness for this reason. Ultimately, a citizen's long-term productivity does not greatly depend on whether they experience a temporary illness. It is thus unfair that sudden, uncontrollable healthcare costs can destroy someone's future economic opportunity. Figure 4.6 shows the share of GDP devoted to private versus public health costs for selected OECD countries, while Figure 4.7 shows life expectancy at birth by country. Unsurprisingly, the US – the only developed country without some form of universal health coverage – is a clear outlier. It has by far the highest health expenditure, and has a comparatively low life expectancy, similar to that of some East European countries. Extraordinary healthcare costs price many Americans out of the medical treatment they need, and often leaves many of them saddled with enormous, unfair debt that prevents them from investing in their future.

Fair universal healthcare systems need not entirely abandon the market. The Netherlands, for instance, uses a universal private insurance system. Every citizen is required to purchase health insurance, but insurers are partly funded by the government and regulated so that they cannot deny anyone coverage, or impose costs or conditions on the basis of an individual's health or finances. Austria uses a public option system, where nearly all citizens are entitled to public healthcare but may elect to additionally purchase private healthcare. Canada uses a single payer system, where the government pays a certain rate for covered medical services but most basic services are performed by private doctors. Where incentives align well, it is demonstrably workable to incorporate efficiency-improving market mechanisms into healthcare, and universal healthcare systems have accordingly been implemented in a variety of ways. What unites these systems is an overarching focus on fairness, such that everyone can expect to have their healthcare costs reasonably covered and avoid drowning in medical debt.

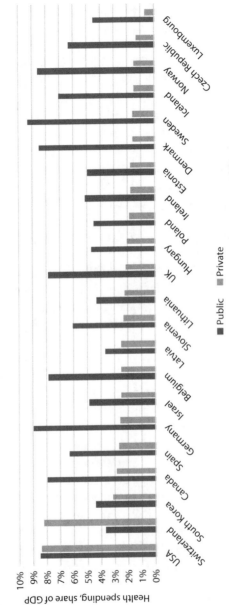

Figure 4.6: Public and private health spending as % of GDP by country in 2018

Source: OECD 2020j

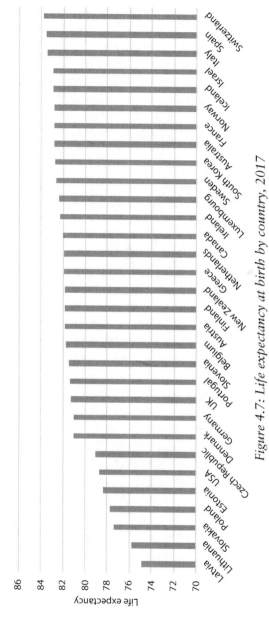

Figure 4.7: Life expectancy at birth by country, 2017

Source: World Bank 2020a

There is nevertheless room for creating fairer health-care systems even among many of the countries that already perform relatively well. While countries such as the UK, France, Germany, and New Zealand have universal coverage of pharmaceutical costs, for instance, Canada (among other nations) does not. A direct consequence is that Canadians spend approximately 40 percent more on pharmaceuticals than citizens of comparable countries with universal pharmacare, and Canadians can still face unfair financial burdens if they become sick and require expensive medication.

Unemployment insurance and assistance are like-wise highly important components of the social safety net that is critical for fairness. Having an employer go out of business or being laid off in a cyclical downturn disrupts a citizen's livelihood, and can unfairly limit their future economic opportunity. It is crucial for the state to smooth disruptive transitions between jobs to ensure equal opportunity with respect to unfair events. At the same time, unemployment protection systems must acknowledge the importance of fair unequal outcomes. Unemployment protection systems should be sufficiently supportive to prevent undue hardship from unfair shocks, but not so generous that people are incentivized to remain on unemployment benefits rather than seek work (see, for example, Lalive et al. 2006).

Figure 4.8 shows the percentage of GDP that various OECD countries spend on unemployment benefits. There are enormous gulfs between the most- and least-generous countries; Finland spends nearly thirteen times as much as the UK as a share of GDP, for instance. The rules of unemployment protection systems are just as important as the funds spent, because specific rules shape incentives. Figure 4.9 shows the maximum duration of unemployment insurance by country, for

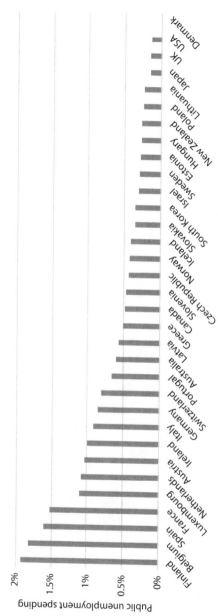

Figure 4.8: Public unemployment spending as % of GDP, 2019 or latest year

Source: OECD 2020k

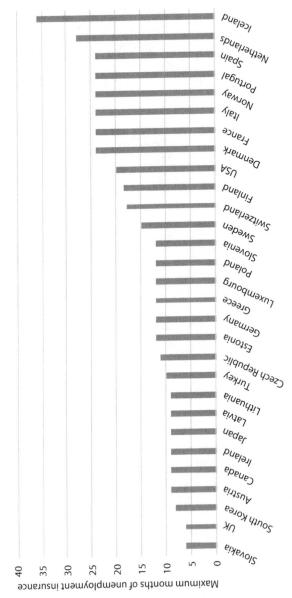

Figure 4.9: Maximum months of unemployment insurance in 2018

Source: OECD 2020l

instance, which ranges from just a few months to two or more years.

Some unemployment protection systems, such as those in the US and the UK, are probably insufficiently generous to support economic fairness. Unemployed Americans must meet stringent criteria to obtain unemployment benefits, such as demonstrating that their job loss was not their fault. A consequence is that only around one quarter of unemployed Americans actually qualify for unemployment insurance. Even if citizens can jump through these hoops, they then have only a relatively short time to find a new job. In some US states, unemployment insurance lasts only fourteen weeks. During economic downturns and in areas with few job opportunities, this can pose a serious challenge and is manifestly unfair.

On the other hand, the pre-Macron French unemployment system was so generous that it skewed toward undermining fair unequal outcomes. Workers could qualify for unemployment benefits after just four months on the job, and retain those benefits for two years after losing it. Around 20 percent of the unemployed in France sometimes were paid more from their unemployment benefits than they were at their previous job. Macron put forward reforms that aimed to reduce short-term hiring, lengthen the duration of work before which an employee can qualify for unemployment benefits, and reduce unemployment payments for high-income earners. These reforms ought to make France's unemployment system fairer by retaining a functional support system for those whose jobs have been disrupted, but cutting away at aspects that undermine fair unequal outcomes.

Norway's unemployment system arguably does a relatively good job at balancing equal opportunity and fair unequal outcomes. The unemployed can claim benefits for up to two years, giving them ample time to search for a new job. However, most unemployed Norwegians receive around 60 percent of their previous salary in benefits, and they must have been previously employed for a full year to qualify. Collectively, this helps support citizens through disruptive job transitions but discourages abuse of the unemployment system that would undermine fair unequal outcomes. Naturally, a wide variety of other approaches exist. Estonia, for example, decreases the unemployment benefit after the first 100 days to incentivize citizens to swiftly search for new work while keeping their finances afloat. Germany uses a system called *kurzarbeit*, where the state pays companies to keep workers on board at somewhat reduced salaries during economic downturns.

Rewarding Value Creation

Even if a country effectively implements equal opportunity – in relation to both personal characteristics and events – a citizen may still be held back by an economic system that does not support fair unequal outcomes. It is impossible for a society to have fair outcomes if competition is geared toward rewarding people equally, or to rewarding things other than productivity. Key among these inputs is that society must embrace rewarding value creation.

Countries range enormously in the extent to which they succeed at creating efficient markets that reward value creation. In 2019, GDP per capita levels at Purchasing Power Parity in 2015 US dollars among OECD countries ranged from more than $60,000 in countries like the US, Norway, and Switzerland to lower than $35,000 in nations such as Greece and Portugal. Sadly, there is no silver bullet to create a highly efficient market; as underscored by Hausmann and Hidalgo (2009), prosperous economies are complex systems that require a huge multitude of complementary inputs. A small fraction of possible examples includes good political and legal institutions, efficient taxation, effective regulation, sound macroeconomic management, and adequate infrastructure. Each of these policies is difficult to implement by itself, and it is especially hard to do so altogether. It is thus incredibly difficult to create an efficient market that amply rewards value creation, which is why there are so few high-income countries today.

A crucial caveat is that it is not always appropriate to view the strength of a country's markets as a monolith. There can be substantial subnational variation, and many commentators today note how "left-behind" regions like the American rustbelt or the north of England both struggle economically and host staunch support for populism. Cities, on the one hand, are highly concentrated sites of economic activity because they contain so many inputs to economic production that can readily interact (Gomez-Lievano et al. 2017). By contrast, rural areas often lag behind because they only have a few such inputs. Depending on the context, it may be vitally necessary to invest in the economic capabilities of a country's regions rather than cities – even if doing so would deliver a smaller payoff in aggregate GDP – for the sake of fairness, so that citizens from all geographies have a real chance to get ahead.

Every country must create the positive inputs to efficient markets in order to achieve economic fairness, as will be seen in Chapter 5 when this framework is applied to diagnose the constraints to fairness in certain countries affected by populism. However, the litany of building blocks for a competitive market is extraordinarily voluminous and thoroughly covered by the literature on economic growth. To concisely provide intuition, this section will instead briefly discuss certain policies that directly *undermine* rewarding value creation by expropriating success.

A major proposal once put forward by a number of American politicians, such as Bernie Sanders and Elizabeth Warren, is an aggressive wealth tax. Sanders's and Warren's proposals from the 2020 US election cycle would have applied tax rates in the range of 2–5 percent for fortunes over $50 million, and rates ranging from 5–8 percent for net assets over $1 billion.

One critique of these policies is that aggressive wealth taxes are impractical. They are notoriously costly to administer and actually tend to garner little revenue, as it is difficult to accurately evaluate an individual's aggregate wealth holdings in all their different forms. In numerous cases, such difficulties have led to the cancellation of wealth taxes. While in 1990 twelve European countries had a wealth tax, only Switzerland, Norway, and Spain do today. In contrast to Sanders's and Warren's plans, the maximum wealth tax rates applied in these countries are, respectively, just 1.09 percent, 0.85 percent, and 2.5 percent, and the share of tax revenue obtained is 3.7 percent, 1.1 percent, and 0.5 percent. The fact that many countries have abolished wealth taxes, and that the surviving policies apply comparatively light tax rates, is indicative of just how impractical such aggressive wealth taxes really are. They are a poor political solution to a difficult economic problem.

An even more serious problem is that these tax proposals are punitive in nature. Sanders's stated goal of his policy was that "the wealth of billionaires would be cut in half over fifteen years which would substantially break up the wealth and power of this small privileged class." In light of the evidence on the impracticality of aggressive wealth taxes, it seems clear that, in fact, soaking the rich was the primary purpose of this policy – rather than any sort of rational economic calculation to expand tax revenue and wisely tackle the problem of unfair economic outcomes. To figures like Sanders, it is not enough to lift up those who are struggling; perversely, the successful must also be cut down to size. Of course, this position and policy are unfair because they hold that after a certain point value creation should not be rewarded.

A similar problem can be found in France's retracted 75 percent marginal tax rate on income above €1 million. Former French President François Hollande campaigned on ratcheting up France's top marginal income tax rate, which then stood at 45 percent. Following his 2012 election win, Hollande battled with the courts to enact the tax increase, and it went into effect in 2013. It was initially lauded by Thomas Piketty and like-minded thinkers, who argued at the time that the top marginal income tax rate could be as high as 80 percent.

Inevitably, Hollande's tax was, like the American wealth tax proposals, highly impractical. Thousands of French millionaires emigrated, and instead of experiencing a taxation windfall, France's 2013 tax revenues actually came in €14 billion below expectations. Subsequent French President Macron derided the policy as being like "Cuba without the sun." Just as with Sanders's and Warren's wealth tax ideas, this policy was never a hard-headed, rational economic calculation for expanding the tax base. It was instead a form of punishment for the rich, and it undermined rewarding value creation.

On the whole, it is deeply important for a portion of the surpluses generated through success in the market to be directed toward public coffers. Without taxing these surpluses, it is not possible to fund equal opportunity, and society is less fair. It is also most certainly fair to tax progressively. Taxation (by itself) is a form of economic loss, and the state should apply the burden of this "punishment" uniformly across the population. Because the value of an extra dollar to a billionaire is exponentially less than to someone living at the poverty line, it is fair to demand a greater share of tax dollars from a wealthy citizen than a poor one. But no policy should aim to expropriate the fruits of success so thoroughly that the incentives to create value are destroyed. Taxation should never be for redistribution's own sake, but always as a means of ensuring that opportunity and outcomes are fair. Policymakers will not be able to build a fair society, or reclaim the populist vote, through blanket measures that systematically equalize economic outcomes or leave too much for too few.

Disincentivizing Cheaters

The final branch to consider, concerning the prevention of *unfair* unequal outcomes, includes a number of elements that are widely seen as noncontroversial. Almost every developed society sees the need to combat crime and corruption through the justice system, enforce safe business practices (such as ensuring food safety, avoiding workplace injury, and preventing the likelihood of fires), and reduce heavy pollution. All these activities are plainly inefficient and unfair because they generate wealth by imposing costs on others. They probably reduce the overall wellbeing of society. But many other issues are not as straightforward. There are often trade-offs or uncertainties in the economic efficiency of many activities and practices, and the final decision of what to permit can be deeply political. Here we aim to examine a handful of contentious issues that are arguably illuminated by applying the lens of unfair unequal outcomes.

An important example is the stringency of financial regulation. Financial markets are essential to the economy and there is much evidence that financial liberalization can drive economic growth (Bekaert et al. 2005; Bumann et al. 2013). There are obvious reasons why having freer access to finance allows businesses to expand and innovate in ways that would be impossible using only their own savings. Access to finance is critical for fairness because it enables efficient markets and fair unequal outcomes.

But financial regulation that is excessively lax, or is liberalized under the wrong circumstances, can result in nonperforming financial instruments and ultimately financial crises (Stiglitz 2000). The economic fallout of such crises typically creates *unfair* unequal outcomes: it inflicts a recession upon members of the public and may even bail out the financial elite with taxpayers' money. Loose monetary policy used to fight the recession can further enrich those capital owners responsible for the crisis, while fiscal austerity used to rein in public finances punishes everyone else. In the end, the financial elite may not be much worse off, while the general public can suffer enormously. As previously discussed, these are key reasons why financial crises have been repeatedly associated with increased political extremism, including the recent wave of populism.

While financial regulation is usually examined purely in terms of gains and losses, the lens of fairness adds additional weight to the argument that financial risk ought to be minimized. Financial crises are not just episodes of aggregate economic loss; they are profoundly unfair and carry deep political consequences. On balance, it may be worth accepting slower credit growth to reduce the chance of a financial crisis, *even if this results in lower than expected GDP per capita growth,* because that is arguably the fairest policy choice for the bulk of society.

An example of a policy that may reduce credit growth, but, on the whole, is probably fair because it substantially reduces financial risk, is the separation of commercial and investment banking. In the US, the Glass-Steagall Act and the Volcker Rule of the Dodd–Frank Act enacted regulations along these lines. Without any such regulation, commercial banks that hold government-insured deposits can engage in proprietary trading, where they use their own funds to trade financial instruments for profit. But this poses a very serious moral hazard: if the bank's deposits are government-backed, it can engage in risky financial bets and expect to be bailed out if they turn sour. Unfair unequal outcomes result. Financiers can rake in returns from high-risk investments, while society absorbs their losses, including through financial crises.

Another issue to consider is the differential taxation of different types of income. An orthodox perspective on tax policy is that capital income (which includes corporate and financial income) should be lightly taxed to avoid discouraging investment, while the tax burden on income from labor (wages and salaries) should instead be higher. This perspective holds that the amount of value a dollar of capital income creates for society is higher than a dollar of labor income. A number of developed countries follow this practice, taxing labor at a higher rate than capital (McDaniel 2007).

Tax rates on financial income in particular are, in many countries, especially low compared to those on labor income. This discrepancy has been famously highlighted in the American context by Warren Buffet. On multiple occasions, Buffet has noted the gulf between the effective tax rate he pays on his financial income, versus that paid by his staff on their labor incomes. In a *New York Times* op-ed, Buffet (2011) stated that his effective tax rate that year was just 17 percent, while the average for his staff members was 36 percent.

In practice, the claim that each dollar of capital income is substantially more valuable than each dollar of labor income is dubious. As Buffet points out, the top marginal tax rate on capital gains in the US was much higher from the 1970s to the 1990s than it has been more recently, and there was no concomitant investment bust. Absent good evidence that a low tax rate on financial income strongly benefits the whole economy, another issue comes to the fore: taxing financial income at a lower rate than other income sources is simply unfair. Wage workers should not have to sacrifice more of their income so that capital owners can pay less.

The rules and regulations governing competition can also create unfair unequal outcomes, for instance in the way antitrust is enacted. While the fair unequal outcomes associated with legitimately successful businesses that create value must be celebrated and defended, there is simultaneously a critical role for the state in prosecuting anti-competitive firms to ensure that success remains fair.

The EU and the US approach this balance in noticeably different ways. In the mid-twentieth century American firms were liable to be prosecuted for almost any behavior that could exclude competitors from the market – provided it was not provably the result of "superior skills, foresight, and industry" (*United States v. Alcoa*, 148 F.2d 416, 2d Cir., 1945). Nowadays, however, US firms are generally permitted to defend legitimately obtained monopoly positions, provided they do not engage in specific anti-competitive behaviors such as below-cost pricing. In order to prosecute American firms for antitrust violations, it must also be proved, in full technical detail, that they engage in monopolistic behavior. On the flip side, EU firms are more easily designated as monopolies and are often restricted from many practices that US firms can legally use to defend large market shares. Simply having a market share of 50 percent or higher is enough for a European firm to be presumed, by default, to exercise market dominance. Dominant European firms can then be indicted for anti-competitive behavior on the basis of a lower standard of proof than in the US, and in addition face other requirements such as a duty to create supply that meets all the demand they face.

On the whole, this creates a European antitrust environment that is relatively stringent toward dominant or potentially dominant firms, as opposed to an American environment that is comparatively lax. There are advantages to and problems with both approaches. One might contend that the EU's antitrust system could benefit from a smaller focus on market share and a greater one on actual anti-competitive practices. It could be entirely reasonable, depending on the industry, to expect a legitimately successful firm to gain a large market share through a superior product or business model – which could constitute a fair unequal outcome. America's relaxed standards for anti-competitive behavior, however, are more convincingly inefficient and unfair. Philippon (2019) argues in detail that lobbying and political donations have weakened antitrust enforcement in the US. This has resulted not only in high prices – cellphone plans and airplane tickets are notoriously expensive in the US compared to Europe

– but also in diminished investment and productivity growth, while corporate profits have mounted. Unequal outcomes that are the consequence of politically determined monopoly and the abuse of market power cannot be considered fair.

To be sure, there can be a tension between promoting market efficiency and tackling unfair unequal outcomes. A fairer financial or antitrust system may, in some cases, necessarily mean lower GDP per capita growth, and there are certainly more complex cases than the ones we have briefly sketched. The challenge for policymakers is to look beyond aggregate economic efficiency alone and recognize that fairness is a critical policy input that must also enter into the calculation.

The Twin Virtues in Sum

When all the above branches, including all the policy inputs that cannot be adequately explored here, are effectively implemented, a citizen should have a reasonable chance of obtaining a fair economic outcome in life. They ought to be able to become productive, access hubs of economic opportunity, and compete for those opportunities without being unfairly limited by family characteristics or disruptive events. They then ought to be fairly rewarded based on the value they create, and should not have to compete with people who get ahead by unfairly extracting value from others. A handful of countries around the world supply these policy inputs relatively well, and consequently are reasonably fair, socially mobile, and comparatively resistant to populism. But many are not, and even the star performers must constantly strive for greater fairness or risk falling behind.

Equal Opportunity and Fair Unequal Outcomes

A crucial question policymakers face is which reforms to enact to make the economy and society fairer. A typical approach is to prescribe a far-ranging list of best practices, but this is deeply insufficient. Policymakers have limited political capital, and need to pursue the reforms that will bring the greatest benefit for the smallest cost. The next chapter will detail, with examples, how to practically identify the binding constraints to economic fairness that any particular country faces. It will make the case that focusing on just a handful of country-specific policy constraints can most dramatically improve fairness.

5

Constraints and Solutions to Economic Fairness

> All happy families are alike; each unhappy family is unhappy in its own way.
>
> Leo Tolstoy, *Anna Karenina*

If a country requires many different policy inputs to make economic fairness possible, how should it select which areas to reform first? This chapter will detail a diagnostic method, based on the approach proposed by Hausmann et al. (2005), which can be used to identify the most binding constraints to economic fairness that any particular country faces. By applying this method in order to understand the roots of economic unfairness in their respective countries, policymakers and public leaders can offer credible answers to populist political sentiments – and thereby reclaim them for the liberal democratic project. After overviewing how the diagnostic method works, the chapter will provide sample miniature analyses of possible binding constraints to economic fairness in four of the leading Western countries affected by populism: the US, the UK, Italy, and France. It will then examine the deeper political economy syndromes that explain the existence of these constraints and propose tentative high-level policy recommendations. Additionally, special attention will be paid to France to analyze Emmanuel Macron's political strategy. Macron makes for an interesting case study because he rose to power by capturing discontent with the status quo, yet also provoked a fierce populist backlash. Finally, the chapter will close by offering a reminder that even today's most meritocratic, socially mobile countries must always be vigilant about problems that may not constrain fairness today, but could do so in the future.

A conventional yet misguided approach to correcting economic unfairness would be to prescribe a set of best policy practices. After all, one-size-fits-all prescriptions abound in the world of economic policy; for example, the Washington Consensus consists of ten broad policy principles, formulated by Williamson (1990), which serve as the backbone of economic reform recommendations that international institutions typically give to developing countries. The logic behind consistently recommending certain economic best practices is simple enough: copy what the most successful countries do so as to become like them. Prima facie, it might appear desirable to endorse this approach, and recommend that policymakers in all countries target every element of the twin virtues framework presented in Chapter 4.

But as Hausmann et al. (2005) point out, political capital and logistical resources are finite – so no country can possibly reform itself along every desired axis at once. Surprisingly, nor is it useful for countries to reform as much as possible on as many fronts as possible due to what economists call the problem of "second-best" policies and institutions. In a nutshell, the issue is that no economic policy exists in a vacuum. Policies interact with each other in deeply important ways, and the same reform may lift, demolish, or fail to materially alter living standards in one country or another depending on the *other* policies in place. Financial liberalization, for instance, might open up healthy credit markets that spur economic growth in a country with sufficiently advanced regulatory protections. In a different nation with cloudy regulatory regimes and rampant corruption, however, financial liberalization may directly lead to mountains of bad loans and subsequent economic disaster. Or in another country, with such rudimentary infrastructure that there are few good private sector opportunities to invest in, financial liberalization might eat up a lot of political capital without creating much economic growth at all.

The consequence is that, in reality, uniform laundry lists of "best practices" are not very helpful as economic advice for individual countries. Hausmann et al. (2005) instead propose a diagnostic method which identifies the most binding constraints to some economic objective that a particular country faces. Rather than a scatter-shot of dispersed reform efforts, each of which may have positive, negative, or neutral effects, the diagnostic method homes in on a handful of missing policy inputs that, if fixed, would deliver the largest possible payoff.

There are four major steps in the diagnostic method. First, it explores the nature of an economic problem and determines an appropriate question with which to frame the rest of the analysis. In the context of economic fairness, we would argue that this entails identifying which citizens face unfair barriers to success and, if pertinent, how the trajectory of that unfairness has changed over time. In principle, economic unfairness in any given country may primarily affect citizens according to parental wealth, class, geography, gender, race, language, a combination of any of these categories, or something else entirely. In part, this question can be answered statistically: econometricians can use large-scale surveys (like a national census) to identify whether certain demographic characteristics, all else being equal, are systematically (and unfairly) associated with lower earnings.

Even with good statistical information, however, deciding which part of the citizenry to focus on is an inherently political process. A policymaker has to weigh up whether to analyze segments of society that face the highest barriers to success, or widen their focus to include a broader swathe of the population that might, on average, face lower but still important barriers. It may, in some situations, be worth running multiple sets of analysis for different parts of the population that face potentially different binding constraints. For example, American policymakers might want to perform one analysis for working- and middle-class families in the Midwest (a region that suffers from especially poor social mobility and swung heavily toward Trump in 2016, and provided important support in 2020) and another for low-income African Americans across the country. When considering the problem of populism, it is arguably useful to select a broader rather than a narrower net, and work to uncover unfair barriers that many citizens face – lest too many voters turn to illiberal political leaders.

After presenting the relevant data and other evidence, it is helpful to pose a framing question that subsequent analysis will attempt to answer. This question should make it clear who is affected by unfairness, and should ask why that unfairness exists without assuming any possible explanations or solutions. For example, depending on the context one might hypothetically ask: "Why do citizens in the south of the country have a lower chance of economic success than citizens in the north?" or "Why are citizens of ethnic immigrant origin poorer than citizens of native-born descent?"

Second, the diagnostic method attempts to prove which missing policy inputs constitute binding constraints to the problem at hand. We suggest using the tree of inputs shown previously in Figure 4.1 as a framework to search for potential binding constraints, the idea being that each branch can help to organize categories of possible problems.

The key way to show that a policy input is in fact a binding constraint is to prove that it is *highly demanded* and *undersupplied*, as compared to a relevant set of benchmarks (typically other countries) which serve as an approximate, collective counterfactual. This indicates that a particular policy input is highly desired but scarce, so that increasing its supply would significantly improve output.

It is extremely important to show evidence not just for low supply but also for high demand to demonstrate the existence of a binding constraint. Very many professional policy prescriptions rely solely on evidence of low supply – like low levels of transport connectivity or doctors per capita – but we would argue that this is a serious mistake. The risk is that some economic input may be in low supply *precisely because there is low demand for it*. It typically does little good to increase the supply of something that people feel is relatively useless, especially when they actually require something else entirely.

As a hypothetical example, one might try to prove that insufficient access to university education is a binding constraint to economic fairness in some particular country because it critically limits substantive equal opportunity. If few citizens from disadvantaged backgrounds are university-educated but the average returns to obtaining a university degree are quite high, that could be taken as evidence that tertiary education is likely highly demanded and undersupplied – and thus a binding constraint. Increasing the supply of university education would probably dramatically boost the economic prospects of the concerned citizens. In contrast, it could very well be the case that, in some other country, few citizens are university educated *and* the salary premium associated with university education is low. This could result from any number of problems that stymie the economic benefits of higher education; perhaps the labor market is so overregulated that it is nearly impossible to get a job without the right connections regardless of education, or infrastructure is so derelict that there is not much use in having advanced technical skills. In such situations, increasing the supply of university education would not yield many economic benefits for citizens, and it is probably not a binding constraint to economic fairness.

Naturally, this approach invites the question, demanded by whom? Depending on the particular context, it can be useful to search for evidence that a policy input is highly demanded by and undersupplied to citizens, businesses, or both. In some instances a binding constraint directly impinges on a citizen's expenses, often through channels pertaining to equal opportunity such as the cost of healthcare or transportation. Alternatively, if citizens are constrained by a stagnant economy that does not support fair unequal outcomes, it may be necessary first and foremost to examine possible inputs that firms demand, like reduced taxation or modernized infrastructure. Or perhaps a missing input is useful to and demanded by private citizens and firms alike. One could imagine a country where improving education would both make the set of existing economic opportunities accessible to more citizens, and boost business productivity to create entirely new opportunities.

Third, after identifying a handful of the most severely binding constraints the diagnostic method explores a country's "syndrome" – the deep reasons why it is stuck in a bad equilibrium where it has been unable to resolve its most serious problems. It is very unusual, after all, for an economic input to be simultaneously undersupplied and highly demanded. Why, one might wonder, has supply not simply expanded through regular economic or political channels? The underlying blockages, which are typically political, institutional, and cultural in nature, create perverse incentives that prevent these imbalances from being corrected. The syndrome that explains a country's binding constraints to economic fairness, as such, constitutes the core root of its experience with contemporary populism.

Finally, taking a country's binding constraints and political context (informed by its syndrome) into account, the diagnostic method makes corresponding policy recommendations. In practice, unfortunately, the first-best reforms to remedy a particular binding constraint may in fact be politically infeasible. A great deal of pragmatism is thus required to identify the best *plausible* reforms that can address each binding constraint. It may be necessary to explore solutions that are technically suboptimal but are possible to execute in the context of the country's syndrome. A very good example was Obama's use of market-based solutions to deal with poor healthcare coverage in the United States.

Performing a rigorous diagnostic is a very detailed process. Professional diagnoses of constraints to economic growth, for example, typically run in the order of months to years and produce a number of full-length papers. Consequently, we intend, in this chapter, to briefly overview *prospective* binding constraints to economic fairness in the US, the UK, Italy, and France.

143

The point is to stimulate intuition about economic fairness, the diagnostic method, and possible starting points to understand the root issues behind populism in these four countries. Our hope is to begin a conversation so that others will investigate the deep causes of economic unfairness in countries affected by populism, and potential risks in countries that are not, using these tools.

The United States: Constrained Opportunity

The US these days, it is often observed, hardly deserves its claimed title as the "land of opportunity." Its social mobility is among the lowest in the developed world, and its 2017 poverty rate was the second highest in the OECD. Wide perceptions of economic unfairness have, as argued, strongly contributed to the Trump phenomenon and all the disruption it has created.

Crucially, the most important factor that explains rising economic unfairness in the US is the limited life chances of citizens whose parents came from backgrounds of economic deprivation, regardless of other demographic qualities. Hufe et al. (2018) decompose unfair components of US income inequality from 1969 to 2014. At the outset of the observed time period, parental education and occupation together contributed only slightly more to unfair inequality than race. But by 2014, parental economic status contributed more than *three times* as much. The authors explain that "the steeper growth of unfair inequality since the 1990s is almost exclusively attributable to increased violations of the [equality of opportunity] principle and the growing importance of parental background variables in particular" (2018: 33). This is a deeply worrisome trend that directly demonstrates a growing gulf in the life chances between those born into well-off families and everyone else in America. There is, additionally, a geographic nuance to this story in that stagnant social mobility is especially concentrated in the rustbelt (Connolly et al. 2019).

The starting point for diagnosing economic unfairness in the US is thus to acknowledge the overarching relevance of parental economic status and its particular impact in the rustbelt. This is not at all to say that other forms of unfairness are neither important nor nonexistent. For example, Bertrand and Mullainathan (2004) famously showed that equally qualified résumés with ethnically European names received 50 percent more callbacks from actual Boston and Chicago employers than résumés with African American names. Abhorrent racial discrimination is alive and well in America. But vitally, parental economic status is the main axis along which economic unfairness unfolds today, and, what's more, is also the most plausible channel leading to Trumpian populism. Why, then, do Americans who were born into families with low economic status have low earnings?

Unsurprisingly, it would be difficult to argue that this unfairness stems from deficient markets that do not in some way reward value creation. On the contrary, the US has one of the world's highest levels of average income per person, its GDP per capita levels have grown faster than G7 and OECD averages since the 1970s, and it is a powerhouse of entrepreneurship and technological innovation.

More plausibly, there are problems that limit equal opportunity. Chapter 4 touched on the way Americans born into working- and middle-class families face massively expensive barriers to success in policy domains such as healthcare, post-secondary education, transportation, unemployment insurance, and more. There is reason to believe, however, that access to healthcare and education may be especially binding constraints.

American healthcare, for one, is egregiously expensive and undersupplied. Figure 5.1 shows that US healthcare spending per person is well above that of every other developed country, yet its life expectancy lags well behind other countries at a comparable level of development. As an alternative measure of supply that especially focuses on the most vulnerable members of society, one might consider how 9.4 percent of the US population lacked healthcare coverage in 2018 versus an average of 0.02 percent in other G7 countries. The US is incontrovertibly paying a very high price for worse healthcare coverage than other high-income nations.

The deleterious impact of this problem falls sharply on the life chances of citizens. As Figure 4.6 showed, private healthcare expenditure in the US is especially high; in 2018 it was 8.4 percent of GDP as opposed to an average among other OECD countries of just 2.4 percent. Because the private finances of Americans must absorb these large healthcare expenses, and because those expenses often come as unanticipated shocks, individuals' economic prospects can be unfairly derailed by illness or an accident. Astoundingly, medical debt is the *leading* cause of personal bankruptcy in the US (Austin 2014), a phenomenon that is nearly unheard of in other high-income nations.

What's more, American healthcare has gotten more expensive over time. Figure 5.2 shows that, whereas US healthcare expenditure as a share of GDP only slightly exceeded that of other developed countries in 1970, it now dwarfs its comparators. All the evidence, as such, is that affordable healthcare is highly demanded by and

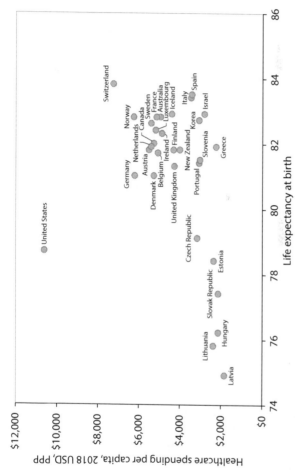

Figure 5.1: Life expectancy at birth in 2018 vs. healthcare spending per capita in 2018 at current USD adjusted for purchasing power parity

Source: OECD 2020d

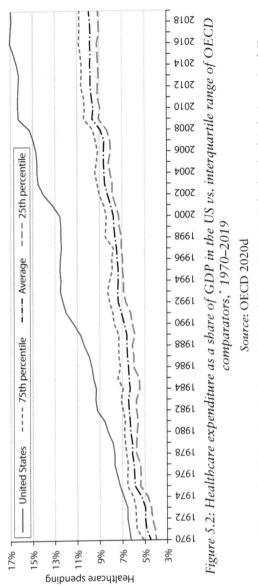

Figure 5.2: Healthcare expenditure as a share of GDP in the US vs. interquartile range of OECD comparators, * *1970–2019*

Source: OECD 2020d

* Australia, Austria, Belgium, Canada, Denmark, Finland, France, Germany, Iceland, Ireland, Italy, Japan, South Korea, Netherlands, New Zealand, Norway, Portugal, Spain, Sweden, Switzerland, and the UK.

undersupplied to Americans who are struggling to make ends meet, and that this problem has grown worse over the same timeline that economic outcomes have become less fair. A lack of affordable healthcare is thus a potential binding constraint to economic fairness in the US.

There is also evidence that high barriers to post-secondary education undermine opportunity in the US. Figure 5.3 shows that the return to tertiary education (compared to secondary and post-secondary nontertiary education) in the US surpasses that in most other developed countries by a large margin. Yet among US adults whose parents achieved a high-school or post-secondary non-university degree as their highest level of education, few have completed tertiary education compared to citizens of similar countries like the UK and Canada. In other words, Americans who were not born into highly educated families would see enormous payoffs from attending university – and yet they participate *less* in higher education as compared to most peer countries. University education is thus both highly demanded and undersupplied. The obvious leading reason for this low level of participation is the exorbitant price of post-secondary education in the US, which greatly outpaces the OECD average (see Figure 5.4).

Though the available data is more circumstantial, it is plausible that reducing the private costs of post-secondary education in the US could improve opportunity by increasing access not just to university education but also to vocational training. As discussed by Autor (2019), demand for medium-skill work has dramatically fallen across most of the developed world in recent decades – with the result that average real earnings for US men without a college degree have *fallen* since the 1970s. Most economists recognize that this is largely a consequence of technological change and

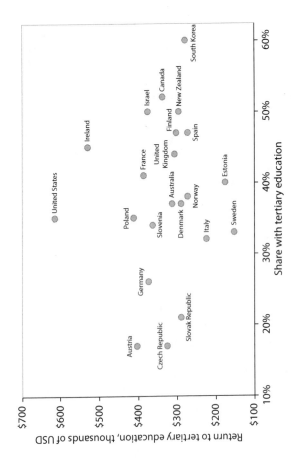

Figure 5.3: Net present purchasing power parity value of lifetime returns to tertiary education for men vs. share of population aged 24–44 with tertiary education whose highest parental education was secondary or post-secondary nontertiary

Sources: OECD 2020a, 2020g

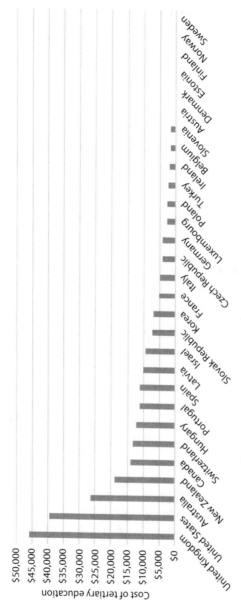

Figure 5.4: Direct cost of tertiary education by country

Source: OECD 2020a

globalization, where tasks that are especially routine and repetitive in nature have either been automated or offshored. Acemoglu and Restrepo (2019) show, for instance, how technological change can displace old tasks while generating demand for new ones, and calculate that the former effect has been especially strong in the US in the early decades of this century. Yet the response to the collapse of medium-skill, routine jobs has not been uniform across the developed world. Figure 5.5 shows that while the US, the EU, and Japan have all experienced substantial falls in medium-skill routine work, the EU and Japan have partly made up for it by increasing their labor shares in medium-skill *nonroutine* jobs.

These medium-skill nonroutine jobs often require critical thinking and unique solutions for different situations, and are thus difficult for a robot or overseas factory to perform. Given that these jobs have expanded in other advanced economies, it is conceivable that there could be unmet demand for them among US firms. There is some anecdotal evidence to support this idea. For example, Autor et al. (2020) note how wages for medical transcriptionists (who perform relatively routine transcription tasks) have declined relative to the US mean since 2001, whereas wages for nurses and health information technicians (who perform more nonroutine tasks) have increased. Some American business leaders also complain about a skill gap in the manufacturing sector; Gregg Roden, a supply chain executive at Frito-Lays, succinctly reported to the *Washington Post* in 2017 that "as we continued to automate our facilities, we found that the talent pool to maintain machines wasn't available."

The syndrome that prevents these binding constraints to economic fairness from being wholly corrected is

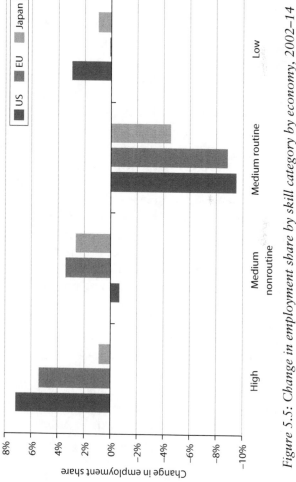

Figure 5.5: Change in employment share by skill category by economy, 2002–14

Source: OECD 2016a

America's profound suspicion of government intervention. A number of historical factors help to explain this proclivity, such as the country's struggles concerning state versus federal rights, the unwillingness of some white Americans past and present to invest in public programs that they believe would chiefly benefit African Americans, the country's central role in the Cold War against communist adversaries, and the anti-statist cultural change that Ronald Reagan enacted. The result is that the US leaves healthcare and higher education to free markets to a far larger degree than other developed countries. This market-led mentality creates best-in-class healthcare outcomes for the rich and unlocks the full force of entrepreneurial and technological change, but concentrates rewards in the hands of the few rather than the many. American workers have thus had relatively little help smoothing over and adjusting to shocks like automation, globalization, and the GFC.

While the first-best policy prescriptions to fix these binding constraints are somewhat obvious – templates for universal healthcare and subsidized post-secondary education abound across the developed world – they are unlikely to occur without a fundamental shift in the American mindset. Due to its syndrome, America will be likely forced to use not just second- or third- but perhaps tenth- or twentieth-best solutions to chip away at these constraints, with the risk that it will not do so quickly enough to address economic unfairness and win back disenchanted voters. American political leaders will need to convince and guide the electorate, and change the language around government intervention to distinguish between policies that promote equal opportunity and those that aggressively equalize outcomes.

The United Kingdom: Left-Behind Regions

The UK is an especially interesting country to study in the context of economic unfairness because it compares favorably on many inputs classically considered important for social mobility. For example, it has universal healthcare, high PISA scores for secondary educational attainment, and a competitive market that includes one of the world's most economically important cities. Yet its social mobility is among the very worst in the OECD. This dichotomy speaks to the importance of carefully inspecting the specific binding constraints to fairness in any particular country rather than reflexively pressing for a purported "best-practice" solution.

Although its low social mobility indicates that citizens who are not born into wealthy families have limited opportunity in general, economic unfairness in the UK is especially pronounced along geographic lines. Growing up outside London or the southeast of England, with a few possible exceptions, dramatically and unfairly limits the economic prospects of a British citizen. McCann (2020) compares UK regional economic inequality to that in other developed countries on twenty-eight measures and decisively concludes that "in the specific case of the UK, the result is clear. The UK is one of the most regionally unbalanced countries in the industrialized world." *The Economist* went so far as to state in 2020 that "other countries have poor bits. Britain has a poor half."

Importantly, the UK's unfair geographic disparities are not simply down to an urban–rural divide – they are a matter of broader regions that lag behind on the whole, cities and hamlets alike. McCann (2020) emphasizes that "inequality in the UK is much more of a regional than an urban/non-urban phenomenon . . . one-third of the UK's large urban areas are actually poorer than their own hinterlands." What's more, unfair regional inequality is accelerating. In the 1960s, London's GDP per capita was in the range of 15 percent above the UK average; in recent years the difference has been closer to 40 percent.

Why are the economic prospects of UK citizens from regions so much worse than in London and the south-east? One possible constraint is a restricted housing supply, which not only drains citizens' finances, but also likely restricts where they can afford to live and holds back the growth of regional cities. Figure 5.6 shows that the UK's supply of dwellings per capita is among the lowest in Europe, and that extraordinarily few of those homes are vacant – indicating a very tight market wherein demand nearly wholly outstrips supply. What's more, the UK housing market is not responding to strong signals of demand. Figure 5.7 shows that the share of household income accorded to rent in the UK is among the highest in the OECD, and yet its rate of annual housing construction per capita is in the bottom third of observed countries.

As discussed in Chapter 4, low interest rates set by the Bank of England are an important factor in the inflation of the price of real estate at almost any level of supply. But the data shown in Figures 5.6 and 5.7 suggest that the UK also simply constructs too few homes. A proximate reason behind this binding constraint is the presence of "Not In My Backyard" policies that hamper urban development, but a deeper explanation is that local governments lack the incentives to cut down these restrictions. There is (as in many democracies) certainly political demand from voters to make housing more affordable, but a crucially important economic

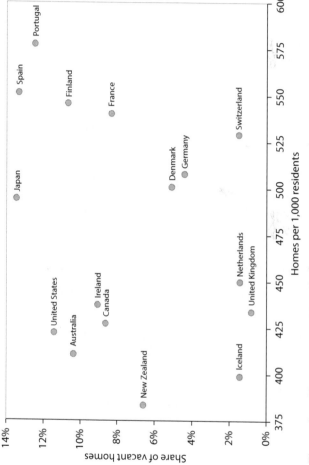

Figure 5.6: Homes per 1,000 residents vs. percentage of vacant homes by country
Source: OECD 2020f

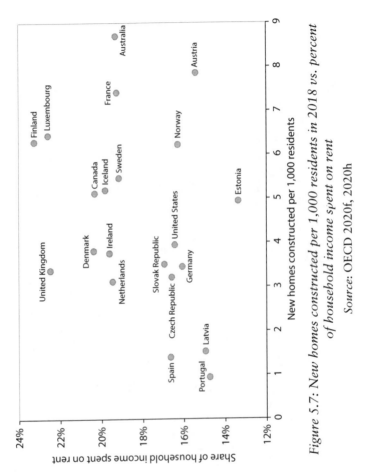

Figure 5.7: New homes constructed per 1,000 residents in 2018 vs. percent of household income spent on rent

Source: OECD 2020f, 2020h

mechanism is missing. Figure 5.8 shows that the UK collects an extraordinarily high share of its taxes at the level of central government (as opposed to regional or local levels) for its population size. This means that UK municipal and regional governments benefit comparatively little from liberalizing real-estate development in their jurisdictions because they will not see a corresponding tax windfall.

Another potential binding constraint that stems from the same root problem is inadequate regional infrastructure. A survey of foreign investors conducted by Ernst and Young (2019) showed that transport and technological infrastructure was the *top* decision factor for investing in UK regions, ahead even of the availability of local skills in the labor force. This indicates that better infrastructure in regions is highly demanded by the businesses that might consider expanding there. At the same time, there is every reason to believe that regional UK infrastructure is undersupplied. For one, government gross fixed capital investment is relatively low for the country as a whole (see Figure 5.9). Even worse, infrastructure investment is disproportionately geared toward London. It is, of course, expected that London should receive more transit investment per capita than regions because it is a city with especially high demand for daily commuting services. But Coyle and Sensier (2019) show that many such projects approved in London had *lower* cost–benefit ratios than projects outside London which were not approved. This strongly suggests that regions are not getting their rightful share of what little transit investment is spent on efficiency grounds alone, let alone considerations of fairness.

As with incentives surrounding housing, the underwhelming political and fiscal power of UK regions likely plays a central role in this prospective binding constraint.

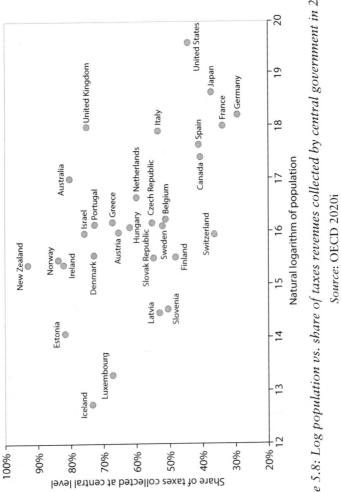

Figure 5.8: Log population vs. share of taxes revenues collected by central government in 2017
Source: OECD 2020i

Constraints and Solutions to Economic Fairness

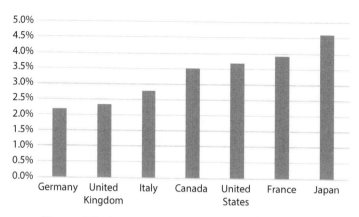

Figure 5.9: Average government gross fixed capital investment as a percentage of GDP among G7 countries, 1995–2015

Source: Office for National Statistics 2018

Figure 5.10 shows that the UK's share of public investment conducted by central (rather than regional and local) government is very high for its population size. If regions had control over a more "normal" share of the UK's public investment, they would undoubtedly be able to spend more on their own infrastructure.

The syndrome largely responsible for Britain's potential binding constraints in housing and regional infrastructure is its overcentralized system of government. No other large rich country collects and spends so much tax revenue at the national rather than the subnational level. The consequence is that an inflated share of national government attention and funding goes to London, and regional governments have neither the resources nor in some cases the incentives to create economic opportunity for their residents. The centrality of London and the political power rooted in the southeast is a longstanding feature of British politics. The modern

161

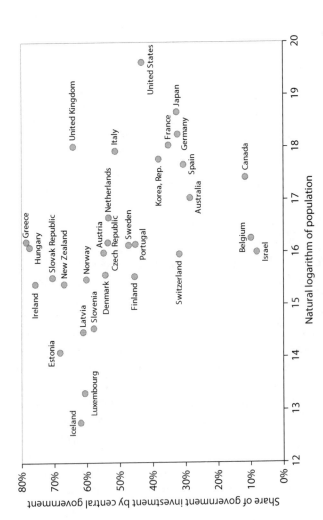

Figure 5.10: Share of government investment conducted by central government in 2017 by country

Source: OECD 2020h

reasons for this are a consequence of the rise of the large centralized state that grew first to defeat Napoleon in the long confrontation that lasted in some estimates twenty-two years (1793–1815), and then to manage a rapidly growing global empire (see Knight 2013).

The corresponding prescription to alleviate these constraints is devolution, combined with increased infrastructure spending generally. Although Scotland, Northern Ireland, and Wales have their own devolved parliaments and assemblies, these subnational governments have relatively little fiscal power; what's more, residents of English regions outside London have no such cohesive subnational body to represent them. A potential political barrier is that devolution has proven terribly unpopular in some corners of the country. A 2004 referendum to create an elected assembly for northeast England was defeated with 78 percent of votes against, for instance, largely due to the perception that creating additional politicians to run parts of the country would be wasteful, especially since those politicians might lack real power. This sentiment was captured by the slogan "More Doctors, Not Politicians" – designed by Dominic Cummings before he rose to Brexit fame. Any British politician pushing devolution across the country may have to carefully frame the goal in terms of shifting power from Westminster to the regions to deliver economic fairness, rather than inflating Britain with extra, powerless members of the political class.

Italy: The Land of Too Many Antiquities

Examining the possible categories of Italian citizens affected by low social mobility and economic unfairness speaks at once to the political challenges they pose. On the one hand, there is an obvious (and infamous) north–south divide in a citizen's prospects for economic success. Working-age employment rates in Sicily, Campania, and Calabria lagged some *twenty-five* percentage points behind the most successful northern regions in 2018, for instance. Income levels in the poorest southern regions are less than half of those in their wealthiest northern counterparts. But at the same time, the whole country faces serious economic malaise that limits citizens' chances of success broadly. Though 2018 employment rates were better in the north of Italy, they nevertheless hovered around just two-thirds – considerably worse than the three-quarters seen in the UK and Germany. Average annual real growth in gross value added from 2010 to 2018 was a dismal –0.27 percent in southern regions, but still only 0.63 percent in northern ones. For comparison, the average annual GDP growth of the entire EU over the same time period was 1.57 percent. It is little wonder that while the Five-Star Movement has garnered many votes in the south, the similarly populist Lega Nord has also flourished in the north. An analysis of economic unfairness in Italy should thus be cognizant of the tension between, and recognize the seriousness of, national *and* regional factors.

Why do Italians from low-income backgrounds throughout the country and especially in the south face such high barriers to success? The severity of stagnant employment and weak-to-negative GDP growth in Italy points toward inefficient markets that do not sufficiently reward value creation. Figures 5.11 and 5.12 showcase potential binding constraints faced by Italian firms. Figure 5.11 draws upon an annual firm survey conducted by the European Investment Bank, and displays barriers to business in Italy versus other EU nations in addition to the US and the UK. Figure 5.12 exhibits

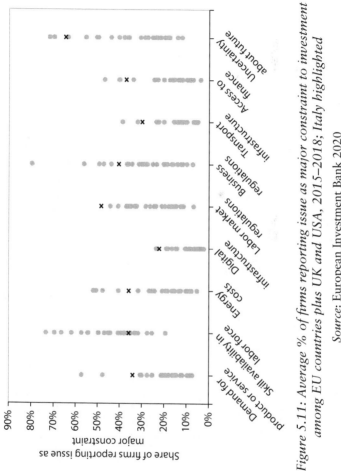

Figure 5.11: Average % of firms reporting issue as major constraint to investment among EU countries plus UK and USA, 2015–2018; Italy highlighted

Source: European Investment Bank 2020

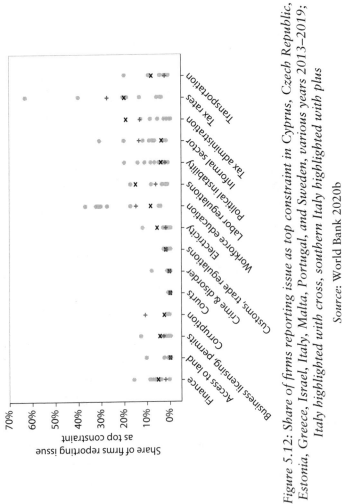

Figure 5.12: Share of firms reporting issue as top constraint in Cyprus, Czech Republic, Estonia, Greece, Israel, Italy, Malta, Portugal, and Sweden, various years 2013–2019; Italy highlighted with cross, southern Italy highlighted with plus

Source: World Bank 2020b

data from the World Enterprise Surveys, which cover a smaller number of high-income countries but yield results both for Italy as a whole and for the south of Italy in particular.

A few general remarks about this data can be made before homing in on potential binding constraints. First, Figure 5.11 demonstrates that high uncertainty about the future is a top obstacle for Italian firms. This is unsurprising given the country's high level of indebtedness and moribund economic trajectory. Many businesses may fear that a financial crisis lurks on the horizon. However, Italy's macroeconomic uncertainty is arguably a proximate problem that results in no small part from its extraordinarily weak economic growth over the past several decades. Only by turning to other, more rudimentary business obstacles – such as the other issues displayed in these graphs – can Italy reignite its economic growth, which is necessary to banish the specter of macroeconomic uncertainty. Second, these graphs, as an aside, help to debunk a common prescription for Italy's lagging economy and poor social mobility: increased education. It is true that education in Italy is undersupplied; its rate of adult university attainment was the second lowest in the OECD in 2019, at 19.6 percent, versus an OECD average of 38 percent. But in the case of Italy, university education is not in great demand. Figures 5.11 and 5.12 demonstrate that Italy does not rank highly in the distribution of countries that consider low workforce education to be a major business constraint, and Figure 5.3 from the section on the US indicates that, despite poor intergenerational educational mobility, the returns to tertiary education for Italian citizens are middling. Increasing access to university education is thus unlikely to be one of the top reforms that will most improve Italy's economic fairness.

A more convincing possible binding constraint in Italy is its straightjacketed labor regulations. A 2012 *New York Times* article gives a succinct personal account of how these laws affected one small business owner, and in turn their incentives to expand and hire:

> In Ms. Pallini's own factory, an employee suspected of stealing had to be watched for two years before being caught in the act. Videotape that had captured his thefts was not admissible in court, so her father and two employees had to spend countless hours gathering water-tight evidence to ensure that judges would not eventually reinstate the man. By contrast, a private sector employer in the United States could have terminated the worker as soon as the theft was detected, unless a union contract was involved or antidiscrimination laws were violated. (Alderman 2012)

While former Prime Minister Matteo Renzi implemented an important labor market reform package in the 2014–15 Jobs Act – he reduced the scope for reinstatement after dismissal, limited the usage of atypical labor contracts like job sharing, and increased the possible duration of temporary contracts – these efforts evidently did not go far enough. Figures 5.11 and 5.12 show that labor regulations remain an unusually salient problem: Italy both cites labor regulations as a constraint at a high rate compared to other issues and is near the top of the distribution for countries that report labor regulations as a major obstacle. Possible limitations of Renzi's reforms include the fact that they did not apply either to existing contracts or to public-sector employees.

The evidence for southern Italy is nuanced but related. Although southern businesses do not cite labor market regulations at a similarly high rate, they do cite one of its direct consequences – informality. One way that some Italian firms deal with onerous labor market regulations is to bypass them entirely and hire under the table. This problem is especially pronounced in the south because Italian wages in each industry are largely coordinated at the national level. Southern firms sometimes cannot afford the wage levels that are influenced by the affluent north and turn to informality as a consequence. The Italian national statistics office estimates, indeed, that approximately 12 percent of Italian GDP comes from the informal and undocumented economy (more than 90 percent of which is, importantly, explained by noncriminal activities as opposed to the mafia). Above-board businesses then have to compete against firms in the informal sector while incurring additional costs. On the whole, then, Italian firms across the country exhibit high demand for evidently undersupplied liberalized labor regulations.

Another prospective binding constraint is tax administration, for which Italy as a whole ranks at the top of the distribution in Figure 5.12 and southern Italy comes immediately below that. Italian tax administration is by all indications needlessly complex. The OECD (2016b), for instance, highlights eight Italian institutions with major tax responsibilities, and writes that the system as a whole is "fragmented across multiple bodies with some roles and responsibilities overlapping." The World Bank's Doing Business rankings, what's more, reported that in 2018 Italian businesses had to spend 239 hours per year filing taxes – the highest in the G7, and far above the average of 151 hours among the other six countries.

However, a liberalized tax administration is not just highly demanded and undersupplied in and of itself. Its absence speaks to another potential issue that the south, as shown in Figure 5.12, is especially sensitive to: the rate of taxation. Italy's tax revenues as a share of GDP are relatively large; in 2017 they were the sixth highest in the OECD at 42.1 percent, versus an OECD average of 34.2 percent. Importantly, tax evasion in Italy is also rampant. The country's accumulated outstanding tax debt in 2015 was approximately equivalent to the amount it collects *annually*, for example. These two facts, coupled together, mean that the tax incidence for Italian businesses which do not evade payment is especially high, as the burden is not spread across a wider set of firms. Given that much of the informal economy is based in the south, it may be that above-board southern businesses feel their taxes pay not only for their own operations but for those of informal competitors as well.

The syndrome responsible for Italy's divided, overbearing regulatory-administrative regime is a fragmented government system that is insufficiently cohesive to efficiently pass major reforms. As a result, many of its market rules and institutions are stuck in the past. Following the end of fascist rule, Italy created a new set of political institutions that were designed to keep government weak, so that another Mussolini could not possibly rise. For several decades this was compatible with the Italian economic miracle. High rates of capital investment, low wages, and proximity to European markets drove rapid industrialization, with the result that real GDP per capita increased nearly fourfold from 1950 to 1980. But as the country moved to the technological frontier it exhausted this model of economic catch-up, and its government system proved insufficiently nimble to adjust. Italy had sixty-five governments from 1946 to 2016, for instance, whereas the UK had twenty-five; this succession of weak, transient governments struggled to self-organize and overcome vested interests among labor unions, big industry, and regions. Unable to reform itself, Italy's growth stagnated and real income per person is hardly higher today than it was in 1990. Institutional factors behind the weakness and instability of Italian government include its proportional representation electoral system, which encourages a proliferation of parties, the fact that its upper and lower houses must agree on all legislation that is passed but lack formal coordination mechanisms, and the limited powers of its prime minister, who cannot even dissolve parliament.

A number of reforms to directly address Italy's binding constraints are thinkable. To reduce the burden of its labor regulations, the country might build on Renzi's labor market reforms and ensure that all jobs, not merely new private sector ones, are governed by modern hiring and firing practices. Ending national-level wage coordination, and implementing it instead at the firm or at least the regional level, would additionally go a long way toward making hiring affordable for southern businesses. More unified tax collection and administration at each level of government (national and local) would reduce the associated bureaucratic overhead for firms, stimulating business creation and thereby employment. All of these measures would help to improve growth and reduce informality, paving the way for a reduced tax burden that southern firms are particularly sensitive to.

It is arguable, however, that Italy must first face down its dysfunctional government institutions before it can be realistically positioned to embark on these labor market and tax reforms. Renzi's failed 2016 constitutional referendum contained numerous pertinent elements: reducing the power of the Senate to concentrate legislation within the lower house alone, allocating additional seats to the parties that win the most votes in an election, and increasing the powers of the prime minister. One reason for Renzi's decisive defeat, 59 percent to 41 percent, was that he unstrategically promised to step down if the referendum did not pass. But his proposals were also marred by the perception that they would increase power for winning politicians – an understandably sensitive issue for Italians given the country's experience with fascism. Tellingly, the autumn 2020 referendum that promised to simply reduce the number of seats in both the Italian Senate and Parliament instead passed by 70 percent to 30 percent. Should the opportunity arise again, a reform-minded Italian government may want to first concentrate on minimizing the Senate's powers, as opposed to increasing powers for other political entities. Such a measure could sizably reduce Italy's political gridlock without invoking the ghost of Mussolini.

France: Espoir et Erreur

Although France has a Paris-centric economy and a substantial immigrant population that is subject to discrimination, its low social mobility likely does not primarily revolve around these axes. The share of France's GDP and employment concentrated in cities of at least 500,000 people was below the OECD average in 2016, for instance (OECD 2018); and while France's employment rate among foreign-born residents was the lowest in the G7 in 2019 (OECD 2020c), Figure 5.13 shows that French citizens on the whole face some of the worst prospects of finding a job in the developed world. The greatest barriers to economic fairness in France are most likely cross-cutting problems that obstruct the success of citizens from all different categories of low-income backgrounds.

Why do French citizens born into families of limited means face such high barriers to success? A natural

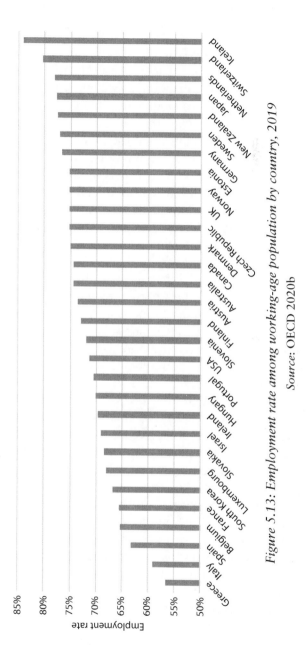

Figure 5.13: Employment rate among working-age population by country, 2019
Source: OECD 2020b

hypothesis would be that the famously expansive French state has not been designed for compatibility with efficient markets, leading to moribund job opportunities. Indeed, if Denmark, Finland, Sweden, and Norway prove that big government can help to create social mobility, France proves that big government *alone* cannot. Figure 5.14 shows that the French state has the dubious distinction of outspending its Nordic counterparts while achieving a level of social mobility far closer to that of the free-marketeer United States.

This dichotomy alone makes France an interesting case study. It is doubly so due to the simultaneous progress and struggle evident in the Macron government's response to that very problem. In certain respects Macron is a role model: he meteorically won the presidency in 2017 with the promise to unblock the most binding problems behind France's economic unfairness, and to thereby revolutionize the stagnant status quo. Yet at the same time, he also arguably contributed to the rise of the Gilets Jaunes and burgeoning support for Le Pen's nativist populism. There is much to be learned from how Macron has targeted France's stagnant opportunity, what more future French governments could accomplish on this front, and the political sensitivities he exposed.

Consider first what France's binding constraints are, and Macron's handling of them. A crucial prospective constraint to more expansive hiring is the stringency of French labor market regulations. Figure 5.15 shows that French companies report labor market regulations as a major constraint at one of the highest rates in the Western world, and see it as a more serious obstacle than most other issues. There is evidently strong demand for simplified labor procedures among the companies that must take on more employees in order for France to improve its economic fairness.

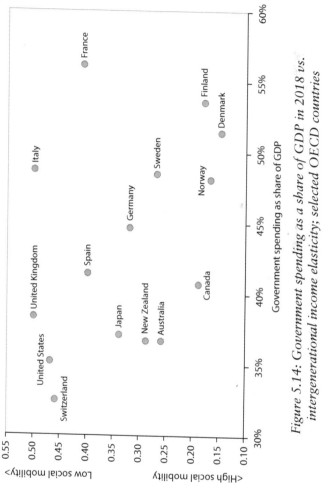

Figure 5.14: Government spending as a share of GDP in 2018 vs. intergenerational income elasticity; selected OECD countries

Source: IMF 2019; Corak 2016

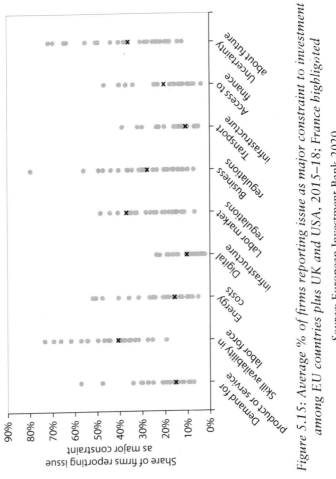

Figure 5.15: Average % of firms reporting issue as major constraint to investment among EU countries plus UK and USA, 2015–18; France highlighted

Source: European Investment Bank 2020

Liberalized labor laws have also been traditionally undersupplied in France, as demonstrated by its Byzantine labor code that runs more than 3,000 pages long. Macron's reforms constitute important headway toward loosening and eliminating these regulations, especially as they pertain to hiring and firing. For instance, the time period in which a worker can challenge their dismissal in court has been decreased from two years to one, the requirements to file such a challenge have been increased and the scope of permissible reasons decreased, compensation for unfair dismissal has been capped, and severance pay has been dramatically reduced. Indeed, Carcillo et al. (2019) calculate that, for example, a 55-year-old worker with twenty years of tenure would have received more than sixteen months of severance pay in 2013 as opposed to just under seven in 2018. Small businesses have also been given more flexibility via new mechanisms to conduct collective bargaining within the company rather than at the union level.

But liberalized labor regulations remain undersupplied in numerous other important respects. In most OECD countries terminated employees have at most three months to file for unfair dismissal, not a year. Unions continue to exercise a strong influence over sectoral bargaining, especially in large firms, and the OECD rates the difficulty of collective dismissal for permanent workers to be just as rigid in 2019 as it was in 2014.

France's extraordinarily high tax rates also constrain the labor market by making employment less worthwhile. *The Economist* neatly captured the challenges the French tax system posed for a Parisian barber in 2017 by noting that "his first 200 haircuts each month . . . pay for his social charges and taxes. Only then does he make his first cent of take-home pay." This demonstrates how excessive taxation undermines economic success for average citizens as well as the rich. Figure 5.16 shows that France collects the most taxes as a share of GDP in the OECD, and that this is largely a product of its unsurpassed social security collection. Carcillo et al. (2019) show that, in 2017, the total tax burden on labor in France (comprising social security and income tax less benefits) was in fact the third highest in the OECD.

There has been some notable progress on reducing social security taxation for low-wage workers in France. Carcillo et al. (2019) show that before 2018 the effective tax rate on labor at the minimum wage was around the middle of the distribution among OECD countries, but following 2018 and 2019 reforms it moved to the second lowest. This change was mostly driven by reducing employer social security contributions and increasing benefits for employees. In contrast, however, the effective tax rate at the *median* wage level remains the fourth highest in the OECD, and approximately 10 percent above average.

While reduced taxation at the minimum wage should help incentivize employment and materially improve the economic outlook of many citizens, the difficulty involved in reducing social security contributions for those at the median wage level points toward a deeper problem: social security levies are so high because they finance France's unusually generous unemployment benefits and especially its pension system. As outlined in Chapter 4, France spent more than 1.5 percent of GDP on unemployment benefits in 2019, one of the highest rates in the OECD. More significantly, pension spending consumed 13.6 percent of France's GDP in 2018, which was nearly twice the OECD average of 7.7 percent. Its average effective retirement age for men, what's more, was the second lowest in the OECD in 2018, at 60.8 years (OECD 2019a). As André Papoular,

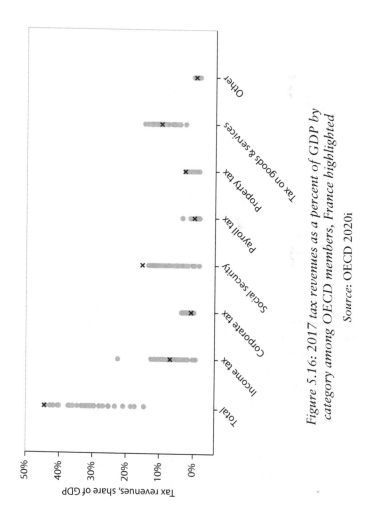

Figure 5.16: 2017 tax revenues as a percent of GDP by category among OECD members, France highlighted

Source: OECD 2020i

Constraints and Solutions to Economic Fairness

the President of Europlane, explained to the *New York Times* in 2020: "The paradox in France is that we have a fantastic social security system, but it comes at a cost. The charges imposed on companies are so high that the end result is that the labor cost leads to uncompetitiveness." Macron rightly declared pension and unemployment insurance reform to be top priorities in his 2017 electoral platform. France will need to make substantial progress on these fronts in order for social security reductions to be fiscally sustainable, and thus to reduce the tax burden on labor.

The syndrome responsible for France's economic unfairness is the fact that, as centrist politician François Bayrou put it, the country "has never been properly *démarxisé*." For instance, the French political left is, according to former Prime Minister Manuel Valls, "haunted by the Marxist superego"; and the country's largest trade union, the Confédération Générale du Travail, is tightly associated with the French Communist Party. These instincts are evident in France's modern policy dispositions – like Hollande's top income tax rate of 75 percent, and the various attempts across numerous presidencies to tackle unemployment with job subsidies instead of liberalization – but more profoundly in a French mindset that is suspicious of market competition. It is no coincidence that French political leaders have repeatedly attempted to liberalize labor laws, and repeatedly been met with enormous popular protests. Like Americans, the French too often do not distinguish between government intervention to create equal opportunity versus equal outcomes. But whereas Americans reject both, the French embrace both. There is, however, some evidence that these attitudes are changing. Grobon and Portela (2016) find that a majority of young adults in France, unlike their elders, believe that social protec-

180

tion is an *obstacle* to ending the economic crisis, and that solidarity is a matter of individual rather than collective responsibility. Macron's election, indeed, would have been impossible without some substantial sense among French citizens that their country requires a new, more market-oriented economic model.

The appropriate set of reforms to rectify France's binding constraints are fairly well understood from a technical perspective. A wish-list might include reducing the litigiousness of dismissal, improving firms' ability to negotiate contracts outside the purview of unions, and simplifying its dizzying array of disparate labor rules. Raising the retirement age in addition to reducing unemployment benefits would further allow for social security contributions to be brought down. Macron's reforms have provided real progress toward a more liberalized French labor market, which strongly contributed to the fact that France's 2019 unemployment rate was the lowest in a decade.

As emphasized at the outset of this chapter, however, any reformer must reconcile the set of technically optimal policy changes with the political reality of its syndrome. This can be an incredibly difficult task, for which France is a notoriously difficult setting. It is also virtually impossible to correct longstanding binding constraints without lively political conflict (that is, after all, why they are longstanding constraints). Macron thus certainly deserves credit for his reforms, both for their direct effects and for their potential to change the French mindset. The most useful exercise is to ask not whether his political strategy has been a binary success or a failure, but what parts are successful and what could be done better.

A great deal of Macron's initial electoral success can be ascribed to his clear recognition of malaise in the

French political establishment; his promise to tackle the country's longstanding problems in a maverick fashion that is "neither left nor right"; and his dedication to do all this in a way that is consistent with France's liberal democratic values. His foundation of an entirely new political party (he in fact refused an invitation to run in the primaries of the existing Socialist Party, in which he previously served as the Minister of Economy and Industry), and his messaging (his party's name, En Marche, indicates a sense of motion; his pre-election book was titled *Révolution*) signified a substantial break with the stagnant status quo. In a sense, Macron thus positioned himself to capture the populist sentiment that the current system was broken and had to be overturned. But critically, he did so by offering ideas that seemed credible to most voters concerned with France's economic trajectory.

Other anti-establishment candidates in the 2017 election, namely Jean-Luc Mélenchon and Marine Le Pen, respectively offered far-left and far-right ideologies. Macron instead promised to convert France to a "start-up nation," squarely targeting the very uncompetitiveness that is rightly perceived to hold the country back. Whereas Mélenchon and Le Pen predictably won 72 percent and 80 percent, respectively, of the first-round presidential vote among self-described far-left and far-right voters, Macron strongly outperformed them among moderates. These voters – non-extremists who are discontent with the status quo – are crucial because they constitute the largest persuadable segment of the potentially populist electorate, much like the key American voters who swung from Obama to Trump in 2016.

Crucially, Macron also delivered on substantial elements of his reform program, as described above. Before the COVID-19 pandemic, these reforms were even beginning to yield tangible benefits, evident in a healthier employment rate. This was undoubtedly recognized by the French public. At the same times in their presidencies, Sarkozy and Hollande generally polled, respectively, as well as and worse than Macron, despite the far more limited ambition of their policy platforms.

Some (much, arguably) of the popular opposition that arose in response to Macron was unavoidable and necessary to confront. The only way a French leader could have reduced the illiberal populist threat associated with addressing issues like labor regulations and pensions would have been to do so many years earlier, when the underlying problems had not festered so much. In other respects, however, some of Macron's policies and messaging proved to be unstrategic. The most infamous episode, that leading to the growth of the Gilets Jaunes, was triggered by Macron's proposed gasoline tax – a measure that disproportionately exacted costs on rural car-owners with no realistic prospect of using public transportation. Though popular with environmentalists, Macron should have seen that this idea was quite unfair to an important part of the citizenry, and that there surely could have been alternative ways to reduce carbon emissions (say, by taxing industrial polluters or airlines). His personal style also comes across, at times, as aloof and arrogant. In 2018, for instance, Macron infamously told an unemployed Parisian, "I can find you a job just by crossing the road," despite the young man's exhortations that employers did not reply to his applications. The critical common problem behind both of these examples is that they showed Macron to be disconnected from the struggles of citizens who experience economic unfairness, which undermined the credibility of his core political brand – and gave his illiberal opponents plenty of ammunition.

Altogether, Macron should be recognized for his success channeling discontent with the status quo toward the binding constraints to greater economic fairness in France. At the same time, it is important to be cognizant of the barriers to political action in France. France's problems are long in the making, and Macron's reforms have only begun to address them. His self-inflicted errors, noted above, did not make matters any easier. The COVID-19 pandemic, of course, also posed colossal, unpredictable, and unavoidable political challenges. Going forward, future French leaders who want to address economic unfairness must channel the energy and direction of Macron's policy ideas, while hewing even more closely in style and substance to the public desire for fairness.

The Complexity of Economic Fairness

Chapter 1 examined a number of prominent scapegoats for populism and the simplistic policy prescriptions they suggest: shut down immigration, regulate online speech, aggressively redistribute wealth. All are partly misguided, and the last is especially dangerous. It draws on a fundamentally flawed debate about how to create optimal uniform economic outcomes for society, by either maximizing the economy's wealth in the aggregate or minimizing differences in wealth across individuals to the largest possible extent. This discussion, and entire way of thinking, is critically hamstrung because it does not ask whether each citizen's outcomes are individually fair.

The remainder of this book has argued that populism is a far thornier problem. It is underpinned by the complex sense of injustice produced by economic unfairness, where citizens (and their families, friends, and neighbors) do not have the chances of success they think they deserve. That broken meritocracy and stagnant social mobility, in turn, does not merely result from one or two key missing factors like underinvestment in education or the ease of starting a business. Economic fairness is only possible when countries succeed on a wide range of policies that work together to create equal opportunity and fair unequal outcomes. Policy failures on any number of those inputs can create economic unfairness. The binding constraints to fairness that particular countries suffer from are thus highly idiosyncratic, and typically stem from deep-seated political, institutional, and cultural dysfunction.

The high-income countries that host strong populist movements today did not sufficiently entrench economic fairness through public policy, and were ill-prepared for modern economic disruptions like globalization, digitalization, and automation. The immediate task for policymakers is to put out these fires and, over the course of the next generation, construct resilient economic policy regimes of fairness and high social mobility. The pressing need to install greater economic fairness so that liberal democracy might be preserved should be a call to arms for countries to address the constraints and syndromes that hold them back. Carefully targeted and communicated, the associated policy solutions could form the backbones of credible reform movements that, by speaking to economic fairness, can reclaim populist sentiments and votes for the political mainstream.

One last thought is crucially important to emphasize: it is not wise to focus solely on remedying meltdowns after the fact. Technological, environmental, economic, political, social, and cultural change mean that new threats to economic fairness are always on the horizon.

Policymakers should, as much as possible, anticipate those threats and proactively search for binding constraints to economic fairness well before disruptions arrive. Crucially, this must include countries that enjoy high social mobility today and have thus far been resistant to populism.

A major example of a possible future challenge to economic fairness is continually advancing automation technology. To date, automation has mainly displaced individuals in jobs that rely heavily on routine tasks. Countries without a social safety net to cushion this blow and provide an opportunity for respecialization, or without a sufficiently vibrant market to create alternative job openings, have frequently struggled with the consequences of that unfairness. Acemoglu and Restrepo (2020) highlight how the adoption of industrial robots has directly caused a reduction in US manufacturing employment and wages, for instance. Naturally, this prompts questions of what will happen should automation further improve. Would a breakthrough AI technology disrupt an ever greater share of jobs that use routine tasks? What about an even more sophisticated advancement that could disrupt nonroutine tasks as well?

A comparable worry is the advent of workplace digitalization and globalization. The COVID-19 epidemic has led to an unprecedented shift to remote work for white-collar employees around the globe. There are some clear upsides to this trend – remote working may improve housing affordability, for instance, and disperse consumer spending beyond large cities into smaller towns – but they are accompanied by the same threat that globalization already poses to manufacturing workers. If a firm can move a white-collar employee from a country's leading city to its outlying regions without sacrificing much productivity, why not simply replace that worker with a cheaper one abroad?

Or perhaps a black swan disaster, like another epidemic or financial crisis, could push a country over the brink. Or geopolitical tensions could splinter the world into discrete trading blocks and shut down many economic opportunities that were once plentiful. Any of these possibilities, or others still, could force a serious rethink of the policies and institutions that a state uses to create economic fairness. Is it doing enough to educate citizens to the standard they require for long-term success? Is it providing enough flexibility in labor markets and an adequate social safety net so that citizens can adjust to new career paths if needed? Is it incentivizing the creation of plentiful, high-quality jobs as old ones go by the wayside?

These are pressing questions to anticipate because even the most meritocratic and socially mobile countries have faced pressure from challenges to date. Markussen and Røed (2020) document how Norwegian social mobility, while among the highest in the world outright, has nevertheless declined over the last half-century. They find that returns to education have increased, yet educational attainment among citizens from working-class backgrounds has contemporaneously stagnated. Although Norway today does not face a populist backlash comparable in severity to some other Western countries, it is evidently not wholly immune to the possible threat of economic unfairness. Perhaps a future shock will derail its success to date and lead it down a destructive path. Every country has cracks in its firewall against the anger and frustration that can give way to illiberal solutions, and all must be constantly vigilant of potential sources of unfairness.

Conclusion:
Scripting a Path Forward

At the beginning of this book we asked, "Is there a script that political leaders who value pluralism can follow to win back disenchanted voters?" We hope that the preceding chapters have demonstrated that there is a way forward. There are a number of clear and crucial policy lessons for any citizen or political leader grappling with the populist challenge.

First, the threat of illiberal populism will not go away by itself. Contemporary populism is rooted in structural economic unfairness that has been almost a half-century in the making. It will not evaporate as any particular politician leaves the world stage. In fact, the danger is that, without a clear alternative, many countries are likely to see new anti-pluralist populist ideas and leaders emerge. This is particularly the case in the United States, which is under intense pressure to address a wide range of complaints but, given America's separation of powers, may not be able to deliver enough. A betting person might think that illiberal populism may further derail democracy. Addressing populism is a generational task.

Second, populist voters must be taken very seriously. Populist grievances stem from a sense of durable and

188

genuine economic unfairness, and must be earnestly addressed rather than dismissed. Demonizing voters as deplorable, entitled, racist, or privileged is a sure way to push them toward illiberal extremes. This is an especially serious problem given the populist view that unfairness results from elites rigging the system against the "true" people. The challenge requires a mindset of *reclaiming* rather than expunging the populist vote. Perhaps only in the early 1930s was there a more dangerous moment that required as much empathy and honesty to address what is at stake.

Third, policymakers must target the binding constraints to economic fairness. This is vital both to win power in the short term and, in the long term, to solve the problems that ultimately lead citizens to illiberal conclusions. The diagnostic method, as outlined in Chapter 5, can be used to identify which inputs constitute the most severe constraints to economic fairness in any particular country. There is some evidence that targeting these constraints is a powerful political strategy to counter illiberal populism. US Democrats found that running on healthcare issues was effective in the 2018 midterm elections, while Macron was elected to the French presidency in 2017 with the promise of modernizing its labor markets.

A necessary corollary to this point is that political leaders should avoid extraneous or, even worse, outright unfair policy proposals. The political left has especially struggled against right-wing illiberal populists in many instances precisely because it speaks to equal outcomes and identitarian "social justice" rather than economic unfairness. Biden won a razor-thin victory in 2020 in no small part, for instance, because the left wing of his party did not differentiate between the popularity of healthcare reform and far more questionable left-of-center policies like defunding the police or a universal job guarantee. In fact, the former is essential for economic fairness because healthcare helps to create substantive equal opportunity; the latter not only fail to contribute to fairness but arguably undermine it. As was noted in *The Financial Times* in late 2020:

> It is instructive that in California, where no ethnic group has a majority, voters went heavily for Mr Biden but emphatically rejected a measure to allow the state's public bodies to engage in affirmative action. Yet in Florida, which Mr Trump won, voters strongly endorsed a measure to raise the minimum wage to $15. Together these results should tell the Democrats to focus on the economic woes that Americans have in common, rather than moral grandstanding. There should be no trade-off between promoting diversity and confronting economic fairness. (Luce 2020)

It cannot be overstated how important it is for liberal politicians to get off the bandwagon of equal outcomes and identity politics and talk about fairness instead.

Getting past these kinds of ruinous misunderstandings requires comprehending that enforced equal outcomes are simply unfair. All the evidence is that, on the whole, voters prize fairness but are deeply opposed to equalized outcomes. Mixing up these two ideas has historically given a path to power for many leaders who believe in neither. It is particularly worth differentiating between equal opportunity and equality of outcome, which far too often are incorrectly conflated. Opportunity is a function of what a society provides so that citizens can live their lives as much as possible on their own terms. Outcomes are the consequence of the pursuit of those life chances. Millions of people pursuing their own paths will, by any understanding of the human condition, inevitably lead to very unequal outcomes. This is a good thing. Economic fairness is more likely when societies promote both equal opportunity and fair unequal outcomes. Economic unfairness results when societies fail to provide equal opportunity, try to make outcomes equal, or permit unfair outcomes where one citizen prospers by undermining the opportunities of another.

Fourth, policy proposals must be directly communicated in terms of fairness and social mobility to connect with the electorate. Illiberal populist politicians frequently rouse voters with talk of a tilted playing field; there is no reason why mainstream political voices cannot do the same, but through watertight logic rather than emotive outrage. Precisely linking constraints like (depending on the country) unaffordable healthcare or the impossibility of getting a good job to a voter's personal life experience of unfulfilled potential could, with the right execution, be considerably more convincing than generic anger at foreigners and elites. Instead of tip-toeing around illiberal populist arguments, the mainstream may find it more effective to beat them at their own game. The message must be that we are all better off when everyone has a fair chance at success, but equally that the fruits of success must accrue to those who earned them in fair measure.

Fifth, political leaders must be aware of both the cultural and the economic sensitivities of the would-be populist electorate. Immigration, for instance, is a notoriously salient issue in modern-day culture wars, and one on which populist leaders take decidedly illiberal positions. Mainstream voices must approach such topics with pragmatism to put out rather than to stoke fires. They should aim to succinctly rebut illiberal ideas without pouring vitriol on their opponents, and then move on. Or one might look at how Macron failed in the design and communication of one of his key environmental proposals, the gasoline tax hike that spawned the Gilets Jaunes. He undoubtedly should have been sensitive to how this policy would be perceived as unfair by struggling rural voters. The same greenhouse gas reduction might have been achieved through taxing more affluent polluters, thereby burnishing his environmentalist credentials without the associated political fallout. By contrast, Canadian Prime Minister Justin Trudeau's large and widely praised carbon tax increase was positioned as fair for the wellbeing of future generations, and as revenue-neutral because the taxes raised would be returned to lower- and middle-income households.

Finally, policymakers can never let their guard down against unfairness. Any number of shocks from technological, environmental, economic, political, social, and cultural change can force a society to reassess the rules and policy inputs that shape its sense of fairness. The most successful societies nimbly navigate new challenges, adjust course, and ultimately pass on their cultural genes many generations into the future. The least are extinguished in violent collapse or slowly crumble into dust, leaving the lonely archeologist to rediscover them, and wonder what happened.

References

Acemoglu, Daron, and Pascual Restrepo. 2019. "Automation and new tasks: How technology displaces and reinstates labor." *Journal of Economic Perspectives* 33.2: 3–30.

Acemoglu, Daron, and Pascual Restrepo. 2020. "Robots and jobs: Evidence from US labor markets." *Journal of Political Economy* 128.6: 2188–2244.

Acemoglu, Daron, and James A. Robinson. 2012. *Why Nations Fail: The Origins of Power, Prosperity, and Poverty*. Crown Business.

Acemoglu, Daron, and James A. Robinson. 2020. *The Narrow Corridor: States, Societies, and the Fate of Liberty*. Penguin Books.

Acemoglu, Daron, Simon Johnson, and James Robinson. 2005. "The rise of Europe: Atlantic trade, institutional change, and economic growth." *American Economic Review* 95.3: 546–579.

Acemoglu, Daron, David Autor, David Dorn, Gordon H. Hanson, and Brendan Price. 2016. "Import competition and the great US employment sag of the 2000s." *Journal of Labor Economics* 34.S1: S141–S198.

Aksoy, Cevat G., Sergei Guriev, and Daniel S. Treisman. 2018. "Globalization, government popularity, and the great skill divide." Working Paper 25062. National Bureau of Economic Research.

Alderman, Liz. 2012. "Italy wrestles with rewriting its stifling labor laws." *New York Times*, August 10.

Alderman, Liz. 2020. "France thought it could reverse globalization, but it's still bleeding jobs." *New York Times*, November 30.

Alesina, Alberto, Armando Miano, and Stefanie Stantcheva. 2018. "Immigration and redistribution." Working Paper 24733. National Bureau of Economic Research.

Alesina, Alberto, Stefanie Stantcheva, and Edoardo Teso. 2018. "Intergenerational mobility and preferences for redistribution." *American Economic Review* 108.2: 521–54.

Austin, Daniel. 2014. "Medical debt as a cause of consumer bankruptcy." *Maine Law Review* 67: 1.

Autor, David. 2019. "Work of the past, work of the future." Working Paper 25588. National Bureau of Economic Research.

Autor, David, David Dorn, and Gordon H. Hanson. 2016. "The China shock: Learning from labor-market adjustment to large changes in trade." *Annual Review of Economics* 8: 205–240.

Autor, David, David Dorn, Gordon Hanson, and Kaveh Majlesi. 2020. "Importing political polarization? The electoral consequences of rising trade exposure." *American Economic Review* 110.10: 3139–3183.

Autor, David, David Mindell, and Elisabeth Reynolds. 2020. *The Work of the Future: Building Better Jobs in an Age of Intelligent Machines*. MIT Press.

Balsvik, Ragnhild, Sissel Jensen, and Kjell G. Salvanes. 2015. "Made in China, sold in Norway: Local labor market effects of an import shock." *Journal of Public Economics* 127: 137–144.

References

Barone, Guglielmo, Alessio D'Ignazio, Guido de Blasio, and Paolo Naticchioni. 2016. "Mr. Rossi, Mr. Hu and politics. The role of immigration in shaping natives' voting behavior." *Journal of Public Economics* 136: 1–13.

Becker, Sascha O., and Thiemo Fetzer. 2016. "Does migration cause extreme voting?" CAGE Working Paper 306. http://www2.warwick.ac.uk/fac/soc/econo mics/resear . . . 16_becker_fetzer.pdf.

Bekaert, Geert, Campbell R. Harvey, and Christian Lundblad. 2005. "Does financial liberalization spur growth?" *Journal of Financial Economics* 77.1: 3–55.

Bénabou, Roland. 2018. "Comment on 'Understanding the Great Gatsby Curve'." In Martin Eichnbaum and Jonathan A. Parker, eds., *NBER Macroeconomics Annual 2017*. University of Chicago Press, pp. 394–406. https://www.nber.org/books-and-chapters/nber-macroeconomics-annual-2017-volume-32/comment-understanding-great-gatsby-curve-benabou.

Bertrand, Marianne, and Sendhil Mullainathan. 2004. "Are Emily and Greg more employable than Lakisha and Jamal? A field experiment on labor market discrimination." *American Economic Review* 94.4: 991–1013.

Bolt, Jutta, Robert Inklaar, Herman de Jong, and Jan Luiten van Zanden. 2018. "Rebasing 'Maddison': New income comparisons and the shape of long-run economic development." Maddison Project Database, University of Groningen.

Broadman, Harry. 2019. "China's slowdown is of its own doing." *Financial Times*, January 30.

Brosnan, Sarah F., and Frans B. M. de Waal. 2003. "Monkeys reject unequal pay." *Nature* 425.6955: 297–299.

References

Broz, J. Lawrence, Jeffry Frieden, and Stephen Weymouth. 2019. "Populism in place: The economic geography of the globalization backlash." *International Organization.* https://doi.org/10.1017/S0020818320000314.

Buffet, Warren. 2011. "Stop coddling the super-rich." *New York Times*, August 14.

Bumann, Silke, Niels Hermes, and Robert Lensink. 2013. "Financial liberalization and economic growth: A meta-analysis." *Journal of International Money and Finance* 33: 255–281.

Carcillo, Stéphane, Antoine Goujard, Alexander Hijzen, and Stefan Thewissen, 2019. "Assessing recent reforms and policy directions in France: Implementing the OECD Jobs Strategy." OECD Social, Employment and Migration Working Paper 227.

Carr, Michael, and Emily E. Wiemers. 2016. "The decline in lifetime earnings mobility in the US: Evidence from survey-linked administrative data." Washington Center for Equitable Growth.

Chetty, Raj, and Nathaniel Hendren. 2018. "The impacts of neighborhoods on intergenerational mobility II: County-level estimates." *Quarterly Journal of Economics* 133.3: 1163–1228.

Chetty, Raj, Nathaniel Hendren, Patrick Kline, Emmanuel Saez, and Nicholas Turner. 2014. "Is the United States still a land of opportunity? Recent trends in intergenerational mobility." *American Economic Review* 104.5: 141–47.

Colantone, Italo, and Piero Stanig. 2016. "Global competition and Brexit." Baffi Carefin Centre Research Paper 2016–44.

Colantone, Italo, and Piero Stanig. 2018a. "The economic determinants of the 'cultural backlash': Globalization and attitudes in Western Europe." Baffi Carefin

References

Centre Research Paper 2018–91. https://papers.ssrn.com/sol3/papers.cfm?abstract_id=3267139.

Colantone, Italo, and Piero Stanig. 2018b. "The trade origins of economic nationalism: Import competition and voting behavior in Western Europe." *American Journal of Political Science* 62.4: 936–953.

Connolly, Marie, Miles Corak, and Catherine Haeck. 2019. "Intergenerational mobility between and within Canada and the United States." *Journal of Labor Economics* 37.S2: S595–S641.

Corak, Miles. 2013. "Income inequality, equality of opportunity, and intergenerational mobility." *Journal of Economic Perspectives* 27.3: 79–102.

Corak, Miles. 2016. "Inequality from generation to generation: The United States in comparison." IZA Discussion Paper 9929. https://papers.ssrn.com/sol3/papers.cfm?abstract_id=2786013.

Coyle, Diane, and Marianne Sensier. 2019. "The imperial treasury: Appraisal methodology and regional economic performance in the UK." *Regional Studies* 54.3: 283–295.

Curry, Oliver Scott. 2016. "Morality as cooperation: A problem-centred approach." In Todd K. Shackelford, ed., *The Evolution of Morality*. Springer, pp. 27–51.

Darwin, Charles. 2004 [1871]. *The Descent of Man, and Selection in Relation to Sex*, vol. 1. Penguin Classics.

Debove, Stéphane. 2015. "The evolutionary origins of human fairness." Dissertation, Université Sorbonne Paris. https://tel.archives-ouvertes.fr/tel-01313145v2/document.

Eatwell, Roger, and Matthew Goodwin. 2018. *National Populism: The Revolt against Liberal Democracy*. Penguin.

References

Economist. 2017. "Just a trim: Emmanuel Macron's employment reforms may not go far enough." October 21.

Economist. 2019a. "Free exchange: Why did the China shock hurt so much." March 7.

Economist. 2019b. "The rich man's world: In Sweden billionaires are surprisingly popular." November 30.

Economist. 2019c. "Thirty years after the Berlin wall fell: Germans still don't agree on what reunification meant." November 2.

Economist. 2020. "Why Britain is more geographically unequal than any other rich country." August 1.

Edo, Anthony, Yvonne Giesing, Jonathan Öztunc, and Panu Poutvaara. 2019. "Immigration and electoral support for the far-left and the far-right." *European Economic Review* 115: 99–143.

Eichengreen, Barry. 2018. *The Populist Temptation: Economic Grievance and Political Reaction in the Modern Era*. Oxford University Press.

Enke, Benjamin. 2020. "Moral values and voting." *Journal of Political Economy* 128.10: 3679–3729.

Eriksson, Katherine, Kathryn Russ, Jay C. Shambaugh, and Minfei Xu. 2019. "Trade shocks and the shifting landscape of US manufacturing." Working Paper 25646. National Bureau of Economic Research.

Ernst and Young. 2019. "Trends in foreign direct investment in the UK's towns." EY Attractiveness Survey, UK, October. https://www.ey.com/en_uk/attractiveness.

European Investment Bank. 2020. "EIB Group Survey on Investment and Investment Finance." EIB.

Foroohar, Rana. 2016. *Makers and Takers: The Rise of Finance and the Fall of American Business*. Crown Business.

Freedland, Jonathan. 2020. "Obama's given the left

a vital lesson in how to talk – and how not to." *Guardian*, December 4.

Friedman, Milton. 1953. "The methodology of positive economics." In *Essays in Positive Economics*. University of Chicago Press, pp. 3–43.

Fukuyama, Francis. 2018. *Identity: Contemporary Identity Politics and the Struggle for Recognition*. Profile Books.

Funke, Manuel, Moritz Schularick, and Christoph Trebesch. 2016. "Going to extremes: Politics after financial crises, 1870–2014." *European Economic Review* 88: 227–260.

Gates, Shivonne, Fiona Gogescu, Chris Grollman, Emily Cooper, and Priya Khambhaita. 2019. "Transport and inequality: An evidence review for the Department of Transport." NatCen Social Research. https://assets.publishing.service.gov.uk/government/uploads/system/uploads/attachment_data/file/953951/Transport_and_inequality_report_document.pdf.

Golder, Matt. 2016. "Far right parties in Europe." *Annual Review of Political Science* 19: 477–497.

Gomez-Lievano, Andres, Oscar Patterson-Lomba, and Ricardo Hausmann. 2017. "Explaining the prevalence, scaling and variance of urban phenomena." *Nature Human Behavior* 1.0012: 1–9. https://doi.org/10.1038/s41562-016-0012.

Grimmer, Justin, and William Marble. 2019. "Who put Trump in the White House? Explaining the contribution of voting blocs to Trump's victory." Working Paper. https://williammarble.co/docs/vb.pdf.

Grobon, Sébastien, and Mickaël Portela. 2016. "Les valeurs des jeunes adultes, leur perception de l'avenir et de la protection sociale. Trois études sur les 18–29 ans à partir de dix années du baromètre d'opinion de la DREES." INSEE.

References

Groshek, Jacob, and Karolina Koc-Michalska. 2017. "Helping populism win? Social media use, filter bubbles, and support for populist presidential candidates in the 2016 US election campaign." *Information, Communication & Society* 20.9: 1389–1407.

Guriev, Sergei, 2017. "Impact of cycle on growth: Human capital, political economy, and non-performing loans." In European Central Bank, *Investment and Growth in Advanced Economies*. Frankfurt am Main.

Guriev, Sergei. 2018. "Economic drivers of populism." *AEA Papers and Proceedings* 108: 200–203.

Guriev, Sergei, and Elias Papaioannou. 2020. "The political economy of populism." SSRN. https://ssrn.com/abstract=3542052.

Guriev, Sergei, Nikita Melnikov, and Ekaterina Zhuravskaya. 2019. "3G internet and confidence in government." SSRN. https://ssrn.com/abstract=3456747.

Haidt, Jonathan. 2012. *The Righteous Mind: Why Good People Are Divided by Politics and Religion.* Vintage Books.

Halla, Martin, Alexander F. Wagner, and Josef Zweimüller. 2017. "Immigration and voting for the far right." *Journal of the European Economic Association* 15.6: 1341–1385.

Harari, Yuval Noah, 2014. *Sapiens: A Brief History of Humankind.* Random House.

Hausmann, Ricardo and César Hidalgo, 2009. "The building blocks of economic complexity." *Proceedings of the National Academy of Sciences* 106.26: 10570–10575.

Hausmann, Ricardo, Dani Rodrik, and Andrés Velasco. 2005. "Growth diagnostics." Center for International Development at Harvard University.

Henrich, Joseph, Jean Ensminger, Richard McElreath,

References

Abigail Barr, . . . John Ziker. 2010. "Markets, religion, community size, and the evolution of fairness and punishment." *Science* 327.5972: 1480–1484.

Hertz, Tom. 2007. "Trends in the intergenerational elasticity of family income in the United States." *Industrial Relations: A Journal of Economy and Society* 46.1: 22–50.

Hessan, D. 2016. "Understanding the undecided voters." *The Boston Globe*, November 21. https://www.bostonglobe.com/opinion/2016/11/21/understanding-undecided-voters/9EjNHVkt99b4re2VAB8ziI/story.html.

Hufe, Paul, Ravi Kanbur, and Andreas Peichl. 2018. "Measuring unfair inequality: Reconciling equality of opportunity and freedom from poverty." IZA Institute of Labor Economics, DP 11601. https://www.ifo.de/DocDL/wp-2020-323-hufe-kanbur-peichl-measuring-unfair-inequality.pdf.

IMF. 2019. "World economic outlook database." International Monetary Fund, 2019-09.

Kaufmann, Eric. 2018. *Whiteshift: Populism, Immigration and the Future of White Majorities.* Penguin.

Kellaway, Lucy. 2019. "My night as an oligarch." *Financial Times*, May 8.

Kenward, Ben, and Matilda Dahl. 2011. "Preschoolers distribute scarce resources according to the moral valence of recipients' previous actions." *Developmental Psychology* 47.4: 1054.

Knight, Roger. 2013. *Britain against Napoleon: The Organization of Victory, 1793–1815.* Penguin.

Lalive, Rafael, Jan Van Ours, and Josef Zweimüller. 2006. "How changes in financial incentives affect the duration of unemployment." *Review of Economic Studies* 73.4: 1009–1038.

Lee, Chul-In, and Gary Solon. 2009. "Trends in inter-generational income mobility." *Review of Economics and Statistics* 91.4: 766–772.

Luce, Edward. 2020. "Joe Biden should beware liberal identity politics." *Financial Times*, December 15.

Markussen, Simen, and Knut Røed. 2020. "Economic mobility under pressure." *Journal of the European Economic Association* 18.4: 1844–1885.

McCann, Philip. 2020. "Perceptions of regional inequality and the geography of discontent: Insights from the UK." *Regional Studies* 54.2: 256–267. https://www.tandfonline.com/doi/full/10.1080/00343404.2019.1619928.

McDaniel, Cara. 2007. "Average tax rates on consumption, investment, labor and capital in the OECD 1950–2003." Manuscript, Arizona State University. http://paulklein.ca/newsite/teaching/mcdaniel_tax_2007.pdf.

Miles, David, and Victoria Monro. 2019. "UK house prices and three decades of decline in the risk-free real interest rate." Working Paper 837. Bank of England.

Müller, Jan-Werner. 2016. *What Is Populism?* Penguin.

Murray, Alexander. 2017. "The effect of import competition on employment in Canada: Evidence from the 'China Shock'." CLS Research Reports, Centre for the Study of Living Standards.

Mutz, Diana C. 2018. "Status threat, not economic hardship, explains the 2016 presidential vote." *Proceedings of the National Academy of Sciences* 115.19: E4330–E4339.

Nolan, Brian. 2017. "Globalisation, inequality and populism." Symposium 2016–17: Globalisation, Inequality and the Rise of Populism. *Journal of the Statistical and Social Inquiry Society of Ireland* 46: 110–117.

References

Norris, Pippa, and Ronald Inglehart. 2016. "Trump, Brexit, and the rise of populism: Economic have-nots and cultural backlash." HKS Working Paper RWP16–026.https://www.hks.harvard.edu/publications/trump -brexit-and-rise-populism-economic-have-nots-and-c ultural-backlash#citation.

Norris, Pippa, and Ronald Inglehart. 2019. *Cultural Backlash: Trump, Brexit, and Authoritarian Populism.* Cambridge University Press.

Norton, Michael I., and Dan Ariely. 2011. "Building a better America: One wealth quintile at a time." *Perspectives on Psychological Science* 6.1: 9–12.

OECD. 2016a. "Automation and independent work in a digital economy." OECD Policy Brief.

OECD. 2016b. "Italy's tax administration: A review of institutional and governance aspects." OECD.

OECD. 2018. "Regions and cities at a glance 2018 – FRANCE." https://doi.org/10.1787/reg_cit_glance-2018-en.

OECD. 2019a. "Pensions at a glance 2019: OECD and G20 indicators." https://doi.org/10.1787/b6d3d cfc-en.

OECD. 2019b. "PISA 2018 results (volume II): Where all students can succeed." https://doi.org/10.1787/ b5fd1b8f-en.

OECD. 2020a. "Education at a glance 2020: OECD indicators." OECD Library. https://doi.org/10.1787/ 69096873-en.

OECD. 2020b. "Employment rate." OECD Employment Outlook. https://www.oecd-ilibrary.org/employment/ oecd-employment-outlook_19991266.

OECD. 2020c. "Foreign-born employment." OECD International Migration Outlook. https://data.oecd. org/migration/foreign-born-employment.htm

OECD. 2020d. "Health spending." OECD Health

Statistics. http://www.oecd.org/els/health-systems/health-data.htm.

OECD. 2020e. "Housing costs over income." OECD Affordable Housing Database. http://www.oecd.org/housing/data/affordable-housing-database/.

OECD. 2020f. "Housing stock and construction." OECD Affordable Housing Database. http://oe.cd/ahd.

OECD. 2020g. "Intergenerational mobility in education, OECD education at a glance." OECD Education Statistics. https://doi.org/10.1787/f143b0f2-en.

OECD. 2020h. "National accounts at a glance." OECD National Accounts Statistics.

OECD. 2020i. "Revenue statistics." OECD Public Sector, Taxation and Market Regulation Statistics." https://stats.oecd.org/Index.aspx?DataSetCode=REV.

OECD. 2020j. "Revenues of health care financing schemes." OECD Health Statistics.

OECD. 2020k. "Social expenditure: Aggregated data." OECD Social and Welfare Statistics. https://stats.oecd.org/Index.aspx?DataSetCode=SOCX_AGG.

OECD. 2020l. "Unemployment insurance benefits." OECD Tax-Benefit Policy Database.

Office for National Statistics. 2018. "An analysis of investment expenditure in the UK and other Organisation for Economic Co-operation and Development nations." ONS.

Pew Research Center. 2017. *The Partisan Divide on Political Values Grows Even Wider.* https://www.pewresearch.org/politics/2017/10/05/the-partisan-divide-on-political-values-grows-even-wider/.

Philippon, Thomas. 2019. *The Great Reversal: How America Gave Up on Free Markets.* Harvard University Press.

Piketty, Thomas. 2014. *Capital in the Twenty-First Century*, trans. Arthur Goldhammer. Belknap.

Protzer, Eric. 2019. "Social mobility explains populism, not inequality or culture." Center for International Development at Harvard University. http://www.tinyurl.com/y2q8rcxq.

Rawls, John. 2009. *A Theory of Justice*. Harvard University Press.

Revington, Nick, and Craig Townsend. 2016. "Market rental housing affordability and rapid transit catchments: Application of a new measure in Canada." *Housing Policy Debate* 26.4–5: 864–886.

Rodrik, Dani. 2018. "Populism and the economics of globalization." *Journal of International Business Policy* 1.1–2: 12–33.

Rodrik, Dani. 2019. "Tackling inequality from the middle." *Project Syndicate*, December 10.

Rodrik, Dani. 2020. "Why does globalization fuel populism? Economics, culture, and the rise of right-wing populism." Working Paper 27526. National Bureau of Economic Research.

Rooduijn, Matthijs, Stijn Van Kessel, Caterina Froio, Andrea Pirro, Sarah de Lange, . . . and Paul Taggart. 2019. *The PopuList: An Overview of PopuList, Far Right, Far Left and Eurosceptic Parties in Europe*. www.popu-list.org.

Scheidel, Walter. 2018. *The Great Leveler: Violence and the History of Inequality from the Stone Age to the Twenty-first Century*. Princeton University Press.

Schleicher, Andreas. 2020. "TALIS 2018: Insights and interpretations." Organisation for Economic Co-Operation and Development.

Sen, Amartya. 2009. *The Idea of Justice*. Harvard University Press.

Sloane, Stephanie, Renée Baillargeon, and David

References

Premack. 2012. "Do infants have a sense of fairness?" *Psychological Science* 23.2: 196–204.

Smith, Adam. 2010 [1759]. *The Theory of Moral Sentiments*. Penguin.

Starmans, Christina, Mark Sheskin, and Paul Bloom. 2017. "Why people prefer unequal societies." *Nature Human Behaviour* 1.4: 0082. https://starlab.uto-ronto.ca/papers/2017%20Starmans%20Sheskin%20Bloom%20Inequality.pdf.

Stiglitz, Joseph E. 2000. "Capital market liberaliza-tion, economic growth, and instability." *World Development* 28.6: 1075–1086.

Stiglitz, Joseph E. 2012. *The Price of Inequality: How Today's Divided Society Endangers Our Future*. Norton.

Sunstein, Cass R. 2018. *#Republic: Divided Democracy in the Age of Social Media*. Princeton University Press.

Tomasello, Michael, and Amrisha Vaish. 2013. "Origins of human cooperation and morality." *Annual Review of Psychology* 64: 231–255.

Tooze, Adam. 2018. *Crashed: How a Decade of Financial Crises Changed the World*. Penguin.

Vertier, Paul, and Max Viskanic. 2018. "Dismantling the 'jungle': Migrant relocation and extreme voting in France." SSRN Working Paper 6927. https://ssrn.com/abstract=3170838.

Williamson, John. 1990. "What Washington means by policy reform." In John Williamson, ed., *Latin American Adjustment: How Much Has Happened?* Institute for International Economics, pp. 7–20.

World Bank. 1993. *The East Asian Miracle: Economic Growth and Public Policy*. Oxford University Press.

World Bank. 2020a. "World Development Indicators." The World Bank.

References

World Bank. 2020b. "World Enterprise Survey." The World Bank.

Yergin, Daniel, and Joseph Stanislaw. 2002. *The Commanding Heights: The Battle for the World Economy*. Simon and Schuster.

Index

antitrust 102
  contrasting EU and US
    approaches 133–5
Australia
  education outcomes 107–8
  foreign-born 25
  income inequality 29
  social media use 26
Austria
  education outcomes 103
  healthcare system 119
authoritarianism 6

Biden, Joe 11, 95
billionaires 30
  American 30, 101
  Swedish 31, 101
binding constraints
  France 174–80
  Italy 164–71
  methodology 139–43
  UK 155–63
  US 146–52
Brexit 12–13, 39
  Corbyn's mishandling of 40
  immigrant stocks 24
  Leave campaign 81

  anger ignored 39
  negative association with
    immigration 24
  as a political movement
    starting in 1990s 13
  as major disruption 8, 11
  Remain campaign 39

Canada
  carbon tax 192
  China Shock 33, 35, 89
  education investment 103,
    106, 149
  foreign-born 25
  healthcare 119, 122
  People's Party 92
  social media use 26
capitalism
  radical egalitarian critique
    87
  unequal outcomes 19, 31
capuchin monkeys (experiment)
  57
China
  impact of authoritarian
    leadership 66–7
  shift to market economy 63

Index

China Shock 37, 76
    impact on Canada 33, 35, 89
    impact on US 19–20, 33, 35, 89
    unfair economic outcomes 71
communism 17, 101,
    cultural gene extinguished 61–2, 63
    equal outcomes 31, 42–3, 61
communitarianism
    contrast with fairness 54
    critique of Rawls 45
Corbyn, Jeremy 7, 40
Covid-19 90
    control for 2020 US election 77–8
    herd immunity strategy and fairness 117–18
    impact on interest rates 111
    role of state 117

Darwin, Charles
    cultural evolution 47
Denmark
    foreign-born 24
    People's Party 93
    social media use 26
    support for populism 92–3
Democratic Party (US)
    diverging values 12
    far-left ideas 40
    focus on economic unfairness 190
    healthcare issues 189
    merger with People's Party 2

England
    2004 elected assembly referendum 163
equality
    enforced equal outcomes

        unfair, dangerous 31, 43, 53, 87, 99–100, 190
    equal opportunity definition 96
    equal opportunity and unfair events 117–26
    experiment with children about fair and equal outcomes 58
    fair not equal outcomes are prized 30
    fairness requires equal opportunity 52
    formal equal opportunity 96–8, 114–16
    how substantive equal opportunity can be limited 141–2
    limits to equal opportunity
        UK 155–6
        US 145–6
    radical equality 42–3
    Rawls's definition of equal opportunity 55
    substantive equal opportunity 44, 98–9, 102–14
    taxation 130
    ultimatum game 58–9
European Parliament elections 9–10, 24, 26, 76, 92–3
    low social mobility and populism 79–80
    seniors in population 27
    wealth inequality 29
European Union 23–4, 164
    anti-competition law 133–5
    medium-skill nonroutine jobs 152
    spending on transportation 113

Index

fascism 7
Finland
  education system 106
  seniors in population 27
France
  big state 174
  economic reforms 181–2
  gasoline tax 183, 191–2
  Islam 22
  income inequality 29
  labor laws 177–8
  social mobility 88
  syndrome 180
  unemployment benefits 125
  wealth tax 129
  see also Gilets Jaunes
    movement
free market 62
  US bias 154
  Washington Consensus 86

Germany
  education system 107
  low intergenerational
    education mobility 103
  pharmaceutical costs 122
  seniors in population 27
Gilets Jaunes movement 12,
  174, 183, 192
global financial crisis
  incompatibility with timeline
    of populism 35–6
  theory for populism 5, 15,
    20–1, 28
  unfair consequences 36–7
globalization 20, 49, 149, 152,
  185–6
  trade shocks 28, 35, 154
Great Gatsby Curve 74
Greece
  left-wing populism 7, 10

healthcare 89
  importance to economic
    fairness 142
  substantive equal opportunity
    99
  transferable advantage 54
  US 146–9, 154, 189–90
homo economicus 84–7

identity politics 5, 17
  amplifier of populism 90,
    116, 189–90
immigration
  amplifier of populism 27
  incompatibility with the
    where of populism 22–3,
    24–5
  incompatibility with the why
    of populism 23
  theory for populism 15–16
interest rates
  benefits to wealthy when low
    21
  housing prices 111, 156
Ireland
  foreign-born 24
Italy
  binding constraints 137, 143,
    164, 167–71
  educational mobility 103
  income inequality 29
  labor market reform 168
  labor regulations 168
  populist revolt 12
  proportional representation
    171
  seniors in population 27
  social media penetration 26
  syndrome 170–1
  system of government 170–1
  taxation 169–70

uncertainty about future 167
university education 167
wages 169

Japan
  medical school entrance fraud
    114
  medium-skill nonroutine jobs
    152
  seniors in population 27
Judt, Tony 31

Le Pen, Marine 7, 9, 12, 15, 22,
  28–29, 79, 81, 182
London
  centralization 163
  impact on social mobility
    155–6
  impact on state investment
    159, 161
luck egalitarianism
  definition 45
  incompatibility with
    economic fairness 54

Ma, Jack 67
Macron, Emmanuel 174,
  181–184
  criticism of wealth tax 129
  gasoline tax hike 183,
    191–2
  liberalized labor laws 177,
    189
  perceived arrogance 183
Matteo Renzi 168, 171
meritocracy 2, 185
Migrant Crisis, European 8,
  92–4
Milton Friedman
  neoliberalism
    incompatibility with

economic fairness 53,
  87–8, 94, 101
  embrace by Western
    policymakers 85
  normative and positive
    economics 41, 85–6
Mussolini, Benito 170, 172

Netherlands
immigrant stock 24
  proportional representation
    8
  universal private insurance
    119
New Zealand
  education 106
  foreign born 25
  health care 122
  social media use 26
Northern League 12, 164
Norway 174
  social mobility 187
  unemployment system
    125–6
  wealth tax 128

Paty, Samuel 17
Poland 1, 16
Portugal
  income inequality 29
  seniors in population 27
  social media use 26
"Project Fear" see Brexit,
  Remain campaign
public transit
  Europe 113–14
  importance to economic
    fairness 98, 102, 112
  UK 112–13
  US high private vehicle
    ownership 113

Index

Rawls, John
  critiques 45
  Difference Principle 44–5, 55
  differences with economic
      fairness 55
  A Theory of Justice 44
  "veil of ignorance" 44–5
Republican Party (US)
  2020 presidential election
      messaging 40
  county-level vote swing 9,
      77–9
  perceptions of anti-white
      discrimination 16
  social media use 27

Sanders, Bernie 40, 128–9
Sen, Amartya
  critique of *homo economicus*
      84
  on fairness 51
Smith, Adam
  Theory of Moral Sentiments
      83
social media
  incompatibility with the
      where of populism 22,
      26–7
  theory for populism 5, 15,
      16–17
social mobility
  country-level variables 75
  definition 4, 73
  France 174
  future risks 186–7
  geography of 82
  Great Gatsby Curve 74
  income inequality 74–5
  Italy 167
  Nordic countries 92–4
  redistribution 90

statistical analysis 76–80
unequal outcomes 75
UK 155
US 144–5
South Korea
  education system 106
  social media use 26
Sweden
  cultural backlash 93
  education 106
  foreign-born 92

Trump, Donald
  appeal, status, and economic
      anxiety 26
  county-level vote swing 9, 27,
      28, 77–8, 79, 140
  disruptive 8, 11–12
  impact of race relations 22
  in-group loyalty 90
  messaging emphasizes
      fairness 38
  right-wing populist 7
  white American support 15
twin virtues of equal
      opportunity and fair
      unequal outcomes
  definition 4, 95–6
  economic fairness 101,
      135–6

unequal outcomes
  economic 18–19, 190
    enforced equal misguided
        31, 42–3, 53, 99–100,
        184
    and populism 37
    stable and prosperous 49
  in education 106–7
  income and wealth inequality
    fair vs. equal outcomes 30

Index

fair vs. unequal outcomes 32, 58–60, 190
parental wealth vs. race in US 72
and populism 15, 18–19, 28–30
and social mobility 74–5
unfair outcomes dangerous 71
US 144–5
Soviet Union 63
surpluses 101, 129–130
taxes, on capital and labor 132–3
ultimatum game 59
unemployment insurance
  excessively generous in France 125, 180
  importance to economic fairness 99, 122
  US inadequacy 125, 146–9
  well-balanced in Norway 125
United Kingdom
  2019 general election 7, 40
  binding constraints 161–3
  centralization of power 159–61
  equality 87–8
  foreign-born 16
  housing prices 111
  housing shortage 156
  immigration 15, 24
  land-banking 112
  public transportation 112–13
  tax collection 159
  trade shocks 20
  unemployment benefits 122
  urban–rural divide 155–6
United States
  2018 midterm elections 189

antitrust system 134–5
China Shock 19–20, 33, 35, 89
composition of migrants 16
economic outcomes 72
economic unfairness
  family background 144–5
  race 144
healthcare 119, 143, 146–9, 189
housing costs 108
immigration 15, 25
income inequality 18
labor markets 74–5
political polarization 12
post-secondary education 149–52
  syndrome 152–4
presidential elections 76–9
public transit 113
race relations 22
right-wing populism 7
savings 117
separation of powers 188
social media 26–27
support for Trump 9, 25–6
tax rates 132–3
trade shocks 20, 33
unemployment insurance 125
values 90
wealth tax 128–9
utilitarianism 44
  definition 41–2, 84
  incompatibility with economic fairness 53, 87

wealth tax 128–9
white patriarchy 116

xenophobia 50, 67–8